THE SECOND EPISTLE TO THE

CORINTHIANS

Christ and Controversy

R. P. C. HANSON

*Professor of Christian Theology
in the University of Nottingham*

SCM PRESS LTD
BLOOMSBURY STREET LONDON

To
THE REVEREND H. F. D. SPARKS, D.D.
Oriel Professor of the Interpretation of Holy Scripture
in the University of Oxford,
with respect and gratitude.

Acknowledgment

To my wife, who gave valuable help in
typing and in counsel at all stages of this
book's composition, sincere thanks are due.

334–00266–4

First published 1954
Second impression 1961
Third impression 1967

© *SCM Press Ltd 1967*

Printed in Great Britain by
Fletcher & Son Ltd, Norwich

CONTENTS

3

II

A FRAGMENT OF ANOTHER LETTER
6.14–7.1

III

THE MAIN LETTER CONTINUED

IV

PART OF ANOTHER LETTER
(probably the 'Severe Letter')
10.1–13.10

INTRODUCTION

THE CHARACTER OF THE SECOND
LETTER TO THE CORINTHIANS

The document known as the Second Epistle of St. Paul to the Corinthians is certainly the most obscure and difficult of all his letters that have come down to us. It raises complicated questions of criticism and of theology which cannot be evaded by any honest mind. It is full of dark allusions and unexplained references the key to which is utterly lost. As we read it, we sometimes feel as if we had turned on the wireless in the middle of an elaborate play: characters are making most lively speeches and events of great interest and importance are happening, but we do not know who exactly the speakers are and we are not sure what exactly is happening to them. And in this case we have no *Radio Times* to supply a list of characters. The consequence of all this obscurity and difficulty is that this letter is one rarely handled by the student, the scholar or the preacher.

Yet it is a great pity that the letter should be neglected, because, for all its darkness, it is an immensely important document. It is the third longest of any of St. Paul's known works. It tells us, even though fragmentarily, more about St. Paul himself (in contrast to St. Paul's *views*) than any other of his letters. To use one of those magnificent words of Dr. Johnson, the very *anfractuosity* of the letter is valuable; its very brokenness, its lack of smoothness, its glaringly unedited, unpolished, unscripted state testify to its utter genuineness. Here, broken sharply off, with none of the jagged edges filed down, is a chunk of St. Paul's life—

authentic, uncensored, bewilderingly complicated, but amaz-
ingly interesting.

Perhaps 'interesting' is too feeble a word; the Second
Epistle to the Corinthians is not simply an intensely 'human'
document,[1] a lurid glimpse into the lesser-known complexes
of the apostle Paul. It is also an immeasurably valuable
part of that witness to the coming of God in human form into
the world which we commonly call the New Testament. This
Letter sheds light on a number of points of the greatest
importance: on the interchange and sharing of experience
which is the privilege of those who are 'in Christ'; on the
apostolic authority of St. Paul; on the righteousness given and
the atonement effected by Christ; and on the function of religious experience in the Christian's understanding of his
Saviour. That is why this Letter is worth studying; we
should rather say, worth wrestling with, because you cannot
study it without wrestling with it. If we are to approach
it at all we must plunge undismayed into thorny critical
questions. But if we can master the main points which these
involve, we will find our labour well rewarded.

THE BACKGROUND OF THE EPISTLE

Corinth was one of the famous cities of the world of St.
Paul's day. Though it was not at that time at the height of
its glory, it must have been very prosperous. It was mag-
nificently situated on a main trading route between the
Aegean coastline and Asia Minor to the east, and Italy to
the west; a few miles to the north of Corinth lay its port on
the Corinthian gulf, Lechaeum, and a few miles to the south
its port on the Saronic Gulf, Cenchreae; in his Epistle to
the Romans (16.1, 2) St. Paul commends a Christian woman
from Cenchreae called Phoebe, whom he describes as a
'deaconess', to the care of the Christians at Rome; she
may even have carried the Epistle. Trade must have been

[1] *Moffatt New Testament Commentary*, Introduction, p. xxix.

particularly good at the time that St. Paul came in contact with Corinth and its inhabitants, because the Roman Empire was then governed by Nero, an Emperor who made himself particularly unpleasant to his own family and friends and to the aristocratic Roman families who largely supplied the personnel of the Roman Senate, but under whose rule the provinces were on the whole peaceful and prosperous. Not for five hundred years could the lands bordering the Mediterranean basin on the east have known such freedom from insecurity as they were enjoying then.

But Corinth was famous for other things as well as its trade. It was famous for its culture, for its buildings, temples, baths, law-courts and theatres, and for its art-treasures, the statues, vases, *objets d'art* and relics of Greek civilization at its classic best about four hundred years before, which had in course of time accumulated within its walls. They must still have been numerous and impressive in Paul's day, in spite of the Goerinesque propensity of Roman governors to annexe them and the well-established custom among wealthy Romans of buying them and transporting them to their villas in Italy. And Corinth was famous for its immorality. Even in the far from Puritanical pagan Hellenistic world of St. Paul's time Corinth had a lurid reputation. Passages like I Cor. 6.9-11 and II Cor. 6.14–7.1 give us a faint idea of what were the moral standards and the moral atmosphere in which non-Jewish Corinthians had lived before they were converted to Christianity. These pagans were obviously very far from the atmosphere of high-minded though rather insipid ethical endeavour (strangely reminiscent of an Oxford Senior Common Room towards the end of the last century) which Walter Pater's *Marius the Epicurean* has led many people to believe represented the normal tone of the pagan world of St. Paul's day. If we can imagine a cross between the gaiety and culture of Paris and the moral standards and racial variety of Shanghai, we will probably be nearer the mark. This association, or juxtaposition, of great culture with great

immorality partly explains the entire absence of interest
in beauty, aesthetics and culture generally which we find
in St. Paul's Epistles, and indeed in the New Testament as
a whole.

The evidence provided by Corinth of the moral failure of
the non-Jewish religions of the day must also have sharpened
the tension between Jew and Gentile within the Christian
Church, which burns so obviously behind most of St. Paul's
Epistles. In estimating the duration and effects of this tension we will find it much more satisfactory to rely on the
Epistles of St. Paul themselves, rather than on the Acts of
the Apostles, because Acts was written quite a long time
after the occurrence of the events which it describes, at a
time when this tension had died down, and its author has
almost certainly underestimated the effect of the tension at
the time, and thrown something of a golden haze of harmony
and mutual understanding over the actions of the leaders of
the Christian Church during the period of St. Paul's missionary activity. But even Acts does not disguise the fact that a
grave tension did exist between Jew and Gentile within the
Christian fold (Acts 11.1-3; 15; 21.17-26). When we read
the Epistles to the Romans, to the Corinthians and to the
Galatians (a group of letters written within a fairly short
time of each other, perhaps two or three years) we find this
tension conditioning a great part of what St. Paul says in
them. Galatians is wholly devoted to the question; I Corinthians makes constant reference to factions and divisions
among the Corinthian Christians which probably had their
origin in this tension; and Romans has the contrast between,
and at the same time equality of, Jew and Gentile as one of
its constant themes; one important section of the Epistle
(chapters 9-11) is given up entirely to a consideration of the
position of the Jew in the Christian dispensation. We shall
see in the course of this Commentary how great a part dis-
sension within the Corinthian church, again in all probability
based on this tension, played.

When therefore we try to reconstruct the order of the

known events of St. Paul's life, we must give great prominence
to two movements which are in Acts treated in a different and
much more casual way than they are in St. Paul's own letters.
These two movements are the opposition to St. Paul maintained by Judaizers within the Church and the raising of a
Collection by St. Paul and his associates from among the
Gentile churches for the benefit of the Jewish Christians at
Jerusalem. Both Epistles to the Corinthians show clear signs
of the existence of these movements. That there had been a
controversy over the question of how much of the Jewish law
was to be observed by Gentile Christians, and that this controversy had at one time involved St. Paul and St. Peter in an
altercation, is quite clear from the first two chapters of the
Epistle to the Galatians. It is highly probable that on this
question some kind of an agreement had been reached or
tacitly recognized between Paul and his supporters on the one
hand and the remaining original apostles, with James the
brother of the Lord, on the other. This agreement would have
laid down a minimum ritual observance for Gentile Christians
(the 'Apostolic Decree' of Acts 15.28, 29), but had not re-
quired that Gentile Christians should be circumcised, even
though it is not likely that Paul attended an actual 'Council
of Jerusalem' (as described in Acts 15) on the subject.[1] The
Collection would, on this view, be a concrete and generous
peace-offering designed to alleviate the tension caused by this
controversy. That it did not end the tension or stifle the opposition from the Judaizers is clear from almost all St. Paul's
letters, and not least from II Corinthians. It is no great
wonder, then, that the years leading up to St. Paul's last visit
to Jerusalem and his arrest there were marked for him by a
two-fold struggle, the struggle to establish his own authority
in the churches which he himself had founded against the
opposition of those who wanted to subordinate Gentile
Christianity to a Christianized form of Jewish Law-observ-
ance, and the struggle at the same time to persuade the Gentile

[1] I have discussed this subject more fully in my *New Clarendon Commentary on Acts*, pp. 15-20 and 153-159, to which the reader is referred.

churches to make a peace-offering to the centre of Jewish
Christianity in the form of a gift of money. Paul had to carry
on both these struggles in Corinth as vigorously as in any
other Gentile church. The Second Epistle to the Corinthians
gives us a unique picture both of Paul asserting his authority
against the insidious propaganda of Jewish Christians and of
Paul persuading the Corinthian Christians to contribute to the
Collection for the Christians of Jerusalem.

ST. PAUL'S DEALINGS WITH THE CHRISTIANS IN CORINTH

The dates of St. Paul's visits to Corinth cannot be fixed with
certainty, and the dates tentatively assigned to them by commentators vary considerably. In this Commentary it has
been assumed that Paul's first visit to Corinth took place quite
early in his career as a Christian missionary, perhaps as early
as the years 41 or 42. We can gather quite a lot of information about this first visit from Acts (18.1-18). We know that
after his first, and only partially successful, visit to Athens,
St. Paul went on to Corinth, where he met with a much
better response, and in a stay of eighteen months founded a
church there; that he met Aquila and Priscilla; that he was
provided with a place for the Christians to assemble by Titus
Justus, and that at the end of this visit he left for Ephesus.
We can reconstruct something, too, of his last visit, made in
the course of a journey from Ephesus through Macedonia
into Greece and back again through Macedonia into Asia
(Acts 20.1-6). It was no doubt during this visit that he wrote
the Epistle to the Romans, and it is quite possible that this
was the occasion when Paul was unsuccessfully prosecuted
before the Roman pro-consul, Gallio (Acts 18.12-17). This
last visit to Corinth should probably be dated 53. We know
that Gallio was pro-consul of Achaia in the year 52; his

term of office could well have lasted, or could well have been prolonged, till the year 53.

It is when we try to reconstruct St. Paul's movements during his last few years of missionary activity in Asia and Macedonia and Greece, when we try to trace his relations with the church of Corinth during those years after the conference (which we may place in the year 51), while he was organizing the great peace-offering among the Gentile churches, that we find ourselves in a region of uncertainty and conjecture. Almost the only evidence we have to go on is that provided by I and II Corinthians. Let us look at this evidence to see what it can tell us.

From I Corinthians we can learn that some time not very long before the letter was written St. Paul had received bad news about the Corinthian Christians from people of ' Chloe's household ', and he sent Timothy to Corinth from Ephesus, probably in connection with this news (I Cor. 1.11; 4.17; 16.10; cf. Acts 19.22). We know of course that St. Paul shortly after this wrote I Corinthians, but we must also assume that this was not in fact his *first* letter to the Corinthians, because in I Corinthians he refers to a previous letter of his (5.9, ' I wrote unto you in an Epistle not to company with fornicators '). And we know that when Paul wrote I Corinthians the Collection for the Christians of Jerusalem was being raised among the Gentile churches (I Cor. 16.1).

Next there are the events alluded to in II Corinthians and the writing of the letter itself to fit into our reconstruction. The fact that it is entitled ' The Second Epistle of Paul the Apostle to the Corinthians ' does not of course mean that it was certainly written after the First, because titles such as these were not composed originally by St. Paul, but were added by editors long after the letters were written. But in fact it is pretty obvious that we must place II Corinthians chronologically after I Corinthians, if only because II Corinthians alludes to so many events apparently unknown in the other letter.

Let us then briefly review the allusions in II Corinthians

from which we may determine where it fits in this framework:

In 1.15-17 St. Paul speaks as if he had intended to visit the
Corinthians, but had abandoned this intention; and he seeks
to excuse himself for this change of plan.

In 1.23–2.4 and in 7.8, 12 he alludes to this same change
of intention and says ' I would not come again to you in
heaviness ', referring to a painful visit he had made to the
Corinthians recently, and to a letter written by him ' out of
much affliction and anguish of heart with many tears '.

In 2.5-11 St. Paul asks the Corinthians to forgive somebody
who has offended; and apparently, as St. Paul says that he
has already forgiven the offender, this person has offended
St. Paul personally.

In 2.12-13 and 7.5-16 he refers to a journey he has
recently made; in the first passage to a journey made while
enduring great anxiety, through Troas and beyond, into
Macedonia; and in the second passage he speaks of the
relief and joy he experienced when at the end of this
journey he met Titus somewhere in Macedonia and heard
from him a good report of the Corinthian Christians.

Chapters 8 and 9 consist of a very gentle and tactful commendation to the Corinthians of the Collection for the Christians in Jerusalem.

In a number of later passages however (10.1-2; 12.14, 20,
21 and 13.1, 2, 10), St. Paul expresses quite clearly his intention of visiting the Corinthian church soon, and, as he refers
to this as a *third* visit, presumably one other visit since his
very first, evangelizing, visit has taken place before the writing of at least this part of II Corinthians.   In these references St. Paul expresses very great anxiety about how he
will be received at this impending third visit.   He also refers
in these later passages to a previous visit of Titus (12.18)
and to some previous visit of St. Paul himself when he
refused to allow the Corinthian Christians to pay his ex-
penses (12.13-16).

The allusions up to the end of chapter 9, though by no means crystal clear, are still capable of being fitted into the scheme suggested by the other references. St. Paul between his writing of I Corinthians and of II Corinthians must have paid a visit to Corinth which he could later describe as painful (this could not be said of his first visit; and I Corinthians seems to know of no other visit). And further he must have sent at some point in the same period a letter written ' out of much affliction and anguish of heart and with many tears '. This letter (which we will henceforward call the ' Severe Letter ') is an important point in the argument. Some have tried to identify it with I Corinthians, but it is morally impossible to describe I Corinthians in the terms in which St. Paul describes this letter. It is true that in I Corinthians St. Paul does allude to someone who has offended deeply (I Cor. 5); but his offence (fornication with his stepmother) could not be described as a personal offence against St. Paul such as that alluded to in II Cor. 2.5-11. Again, there is no great difficulty in fitting into our original framework the journey to Troas and beyond into Macedonia alluded to in II Cor. 2 and the happy encounter with Titus described in II Cor. 7; and references to the Collection for the Christians of Jerusalem in II Cor. 8 and 9 present us with no obvious inconsistency. So far, the events alluded to in this letter, though we cannot glean much information about them, can be seen to fit fairly easily into the period between the writing of I Corinthians and St. Paul's last stay of three months in Greece.

But when we come to the allusions in chapters 10-13 of II Corinthians we find something very like an absolute contradiction. Here St. Paul more than once expresses a clear intention of visiting the Corinthian Christians. How is it that at the beginning of II Corinthians he excuses himself for changing his mind and deciding not to visit Corinth, yet at the end of the work he expresses his intention of visiting Corinth soon? If he has changed his mind again he does not say so. If II Corinthians was sent as it now stands, it must have produced a most bewildering impression on the minds of the Corinthian Christians. This is a major inconsistency to be found in this work. But it is not the only one. There are so many other inconsistencies that the question is inevitably raised in our minds whether II Corinthians represents only one original letter of St. Paul or whether it is not in fact an amalgamation of two or more.

THE INTEGRITY OF THE EPISTLE

The fact is that at chapter 10 there takes place in this work a most remarkable change of tone. Chapters 8 and 9 have been concerned with commending the Collection—for the Christians of Jerusalem—to the Corinthians gently and tactfully, in a tone quite consistent with what has gone before in the work. They end with the words ' Thanks be unto God for his unspeakable gift! ', expressing St. Paul's joy at the generosity both of the Corinthians and of other churches, and the fellowship in God which has resulted from it. They are words of joy, peace, content. But with chapter 10 an entirely different manner of writing, and mood in the writer, begin. We find jarring sarcasm, violent self-defence, fierce accusation of others. In these last chapters St. Paul breathes anything but peace and joy, but rather distress, anxiety and anger. His manner is the reverse of tactful, it is almost truculent. If II Corinthians was written as one letter, then the tactful commendation of the Collection in chapters 8 and 9 must have been utterly ruined by the roughness, sarcasm and severity of chapters 10–13.

Let us, however, glance at a few particular examples of the inconsistency between chapters 1–9 and chapters 10–13. In several places in the first part of the work, for instance, St. Paul expresses confidence in the Corinthians' good qualities, in their faith, knowledge, earnestness and love (1.24; 7.16; 8.7); but more than once in the second part he hints at their uncertainty in faith, and at the existence among them of strife, conflicts and arrogance (12.20, 21; 13.5, 'Examine yourselves, whether ye be in the faith '). In the first part St. Paul declares that he shares the Corinthians' joy, that he glories in them, that he·regards them as having proved themselves innocent (2.3; 7.4, 11); in the second part he expects to have to show boldness against those who are likely to suspect and attack him (10.2-5), he fears that the Corinthians' minds may have been 'corrupted from the simplicity that is in Christ' (11.3), and he contemplates the possibility of having to deal sharply with them when he arrives (13.10). A contrast between the two parts as striking is revealed if we analyse the use in II Corinthians of the Greek word for 'boasting' and cognates (*kauchasthai, kauchesis, kauchema*). In chapters 1–9 this root occurs nine times, and it always means 'boasting' in a complimentary sense—St. Paul's boasting of the Corinthians' loyalty, or some such meaning. In chapters 10–13 the root occurs nineteen times, and always in an apologetic meaning, of St. Paul vindicating himself, or some similar sense. Finally, on three occasions in the first part St. Paul declares that he has no need to commend himself (3.1; 5.12, 'we commend not ourselves again unto you'; 8.8). But in five distinct places in the second part he does explicitly commend himself (10.7; 11.5, 18, 23; 12.12).

In the face of all this evidence—the contradiction about St. Paul's intention of visiting Corinth, the startling change of tone, and the particular inconsistencies listed above—it becomes very difficult indeed to maintain that II Corinthians, as we know it, emerged originally from St. Paul's pen or mind as a single epistle. It is much more likely that what we have here is in fact two epistles, the second one beginning at chapter 10. And a theory has been advanced to explain the difficulties which is to our minds most convincing. It has been suggested that chapters 10–13 are not only a separate Letter from chapters 1–9, but that they are in fact part of the 'Severe Letter', the letter alluded to in II Cor. 2.4 as written 'out of much affliction and anguish of heart . . . with many tears'. This theory would explain satisfactorily all the major difficulties we have encountered. It would mean, of course, that chapters 10–13 were written before chapters 1–9, and the intention expressed in them of visiting the Corinthians would then be the intention which sent St. Paul from Ephesus through Troas to Macedonia, and which was only abandoned (as chapters 1–9 tell us) when he met Titus in Macedonia and heard the good news of the Corinthians' change of heart. Chapters 10–13 *are* a painful letter, a letter written out of distress, anguish and tears, a letter striving fiercely, almost desperately, to assert St. Paul's apostolic authority in the face of a strong challenge to it, a letter actuated by the bad news of the Corinthians' disposition towards St. Paul which caused him such intense anxiety. Chapters 1–9 are a letter written when the crisis has passed, when the good news has reached St. Paul in Macedonia, when St. Paul can with confidence congratulate the Corinthian Christians, rejoice in their loyalty, and (though here tact is obviously needed) commend the Collection to them.

Not only do the contrasts between the first and second parts of II Corinthians, already noted, support this theory— the refusal to commend himself and the boasting only in the Corinthians' good qualities in the first, in contrast to the consistent self-commendation and self-vindication in the second —but there are several points in chapters 1–9 (which we have of course assumed to be the *later* letter) which look like references to the earlier letter, the 'Severe Letter' (chapters 10–13). 'Having in a readiness' (i.e. being ready), he says in 10.6, 'to revenge all disobedience, when your obedience is fulfilled'; and his words in 2.9 seem to refer to this, 'For to this end also did I write, that I might know the proof of you, whether ye be obedient in all things.' In 12.16 he wrote, 'But be it so, I did not burden you: nevertheless, being crafty, I caught you with guile'; and in 4.2 he seems to be remembering this accusation: 'But (we) have renounced the hidden things of dishonesty, not walking in craftiness, nor handling the word of God deceitfully; but by manifestation of the truth commending ourselves to every man's conscience in the sight of God.' In 13.2 he says, 'I told you before . . . which heretofore have sinned, and to all other, that if I come again, I will not spare.' He is surely referring to this in 1.23 when he says, 'Moreover I call God for a record upon my soul, that to spare you I came not as yet unto Corinth.' Finally his phrase in 5.13, 'For whether we be beside ourselves, it is to God', sounds as if it may well refer to his 'Severe Letter', chapters 10–13, in which at one or two points he verges upon the hysterical.

We have therefore assumed in this Commentary that chapters 10.1–13.10 are not part of the rest of II Corinthians but are part (perhaps the concluding part) of the 'Severe Letter', and we have taken them as a separate letter. We have assumed, for reasons which will appear presently, that 13.11-14 are part of the later letter, and should be attached to 9.15, to form that letter's conclusion. We have also assumed, for reasons that will be explained in the Commentary proper, that the passage 6.14–7.1 is a fragment belonging to some other letter, neither the 'Severe Letter' nor the letter that followed it (chapters 1-9), but some other (possibly the one referred to in I Corinthians 5.9).

HOW THESE LETTERS BECAME CONNECTED

The assumption that chapters 10–13 of II Corinthians are part of the 'Severe Letter' has not received the approval of all scholars. Some explain the remarkable contrast in tone between the first and the second part of the work by saying that the first part is addressed to the Corinthian Christians as a whole, and approves only some of their actions, whereas the second is addressed only to the party who were opposing St. Paul; the apostle changes his tone with the change of subject. The sharpness of the contrast found within the same letter is accounted for by reference to Oriental exaggeration and to St. Paul's temperament. On the other hand they point out that even in chapters 1–9 St. Paul assumes that some of the evils attacked in chapters 10–13 are rife, the slanders on his character, the corruption of the gospel; if chapters 10–13 are the ' Severe Letter ', it obviously was not completely successful in its purpose. They therefore assume that the ' Severe Letter ' mentioned some quite different offences, and had no connection with chapters 10–13.

We have not, however, found these arguments at all adequate to account for the inconsistencies to be found in II Corinthians, or strong enough to shake the theory that chapters 10–13 represent part of the ' Severe Letter '. St. Paul's temperament would have to be almost schizophrenic to produce in one letter the change observable after chapter 9, and Oriental exaggeration cannot explain sheer contradictions. Temperament and exaggeration, however, could well explain the fact that in chapters 1–9 (the later letter) St. Paul expresses himself as so very well pleased with the Corinthians, even though it is obvious that the offences attacked so vigorously in chapter 10–13 (the earlier letter) have not yet been completely suppressed.

There is one more objection which has been advanced against the theory adopted here, and it is one which we must take more seriously, because our consideration of it will bring us far in our understanding of how the connection of the two letters could have taken place. If II Corinthians is really two letters which were originally separate, how is it that there is no manuscript evidence to support this theory? How is it that none of the existing early copies of this work suggest by disturbance or confusion at the beginning of chapter 10, or by any other way, that chapters 10–13 were originally separate? This is just the sort of evidence we should expect to find pointing to such a theory, but in fact it is completely lacking.

The answer to this perfectly reasonable objection is that we must try to envisage the circumstances in which II Corinthians, as we now know it, was first published generally among Christian churches and began to be widely copied and regarded as worth reading and studying. I Corinthians was known and copied and quoted quickly and early. Clement of Rome, writing about A.D. 96, knows it. But II Corinthians was published and widely recognized only comparatively late. Polycarp and Marcion, at the end of the first half of the second century, are the first to refer to it; Irenaeus (c. 180) is the first to call it 'the second letter of Paul to the Corinthians'. Suppose that during the first thirty years of the second century churches begin searching their archives for letters written by St. Paul. Paul has by now become a recognized and venerated figure of the past, and is no longer a recent and rather controversial claimant to apostolic authority, as he certainly was in the eyes of many Christians during his lifetime and for many years afterwards. Suppose the Christians of Corinth find in their archives— kept, perhaps, at the house of a leading Christian, or of the descendants of one of the earliest Christians in Corinth— three letters, one complete (II Cor. 1–9), one incomplete (II Cor. 10–13), and one (II Cor. 6.14–7.1) a mere fragment of 111 words rolled up in the roll containing the longest of the three letters. These are letters from the great apostle Paul to the church of Corinth which he founded; they are to be cherished, read at public worship and circulated among Christians with reverence and pride. But one is a tiny fragment and another has no beginning or ending and is far from complimentary to the Christians of Corinth. Are the leaders of the Corinthian church to admit that they have allowed the great Apostle's letters to be lost in part, and are they to circulate them mutilated and unedited? No: the obvious thing to do is for them to publish all three as one letter, instructing their scribe to copy the second longest one at the end of the longest, but to make the last few valedictory verses of the longest serve as the valedictory verses of the second also, and to interpolate the tiny fragment in that part of the longest letter where it happened to be rolled up with it. The Second Epistle of Paul to the Corinthians would then emerge as a presentable, though rather obscure, and on the whole not uncomplimentary composition. Unless by some miracle the autographs (that is, the original letters as they left St. Paul's hand, or that of his scribe) of all three letters had been preserved, there would of course be no manuscript evidence to betray this amalgamation. Some such supposition as this would account for II Corinthians being composed of two letters (and a fragment); it seems to us an eminently reasonable supposition.

If this splitting up of a book of the New Testament and an epistle of the great St. Paul shocks and disturbs some, they should consider what exactly they expect the books of the New Testament to be. If the gospels and epistles are regarded as oracles, inspired books full of mysterious wisdom, then of course it is very disconcerting to find them divided up in this way and analysed into originally separate fragments. It would be much more satisfactory if they could be regarded as carefully composed works revised and completed to the last detail with the Holy Spirit as a sort of general editor. In fact, however, this is a completely untrue account of any book of the New Testament, indeed of any book of the Bible. The custom of treating the books of the Bible as if they were oracles, or even divine cross-word puzzles, sprang up in most cases long after the books were written. Even the people who first published them and circulated them did not regard them primarily as inspired oracles. They regarded them as *witness*. The books of the New Testament should not stand or fall in our estimation by whether they are inspired, but rather by whether they constitute early, authentic, original and unique witness to, evidence for, the coming of Jesus the Christ into the world to redeem it. And it is obvious that whereas oracles are gravely impaired in their effectiveness if we can apply source-criticism to them, witness and evidence are not at all affected by such an experiment. If you read John Hersey's book *Hiroshima,* you will find no difficulty at all in applying source-criticism to it; its account of the explosion of the atomic bomb in Hiroshima is manifestly composed from the stories of several different people—a typist, a doctor, a Methodist minister, a Jesuit priest, and so on. These stories in some minor points contradict each other, and none of them pretends to tell the whole story of the explosion. They are early, authentic, unique accounts of eye-witnesses; that is all. But they serve to build up a magnificent picture of what happened. The same is true of the books of the New Testament. They constitute eye-witnesses' accounts of the vastly more important irruption of the Word of God into flesh, and for that reason they too are vastly important. But that does not prevent their being at the same time in many places unpolished, inconsistent, with many jagged edges and unresolved contradictions, and full of local, particular and to us unimportant preoccupations and prejudices. Evidence is almost always of this character. The evidence provided by II Corinthians is no exception.

THE DATE OF II CORINTHIANS

There is one more point about II Corinthians which we have not yet discussed, and that is the date of its writing. As has been made clear, it is impossible to be certain of the exact date of either letter in this work, though the limits within which it must be placed are clear, somewhere between 51 and 53. The first part must have been written in the autumn of the year in the spring of which I Corinthians was written (as St. Paul's reference to the Passover in I Cor. 5.6-8 shows), and the second part only a few weeks before the first. We will probably be not very far wrong if we place the writing of both letters in the year 52. The 'Severe Letter' was probably written from Ephesus, the other was certainly written from Macedonia.

To end this Introduction we give a reconstruction of St. Paul's movements between his first visit to Corinth and his last, divided into nine stages.

(i) St. Paul visits Corinth for the first time, founds a church there, meets Aquila and Priscilla, etc. A year and six months later he leaves for Ephesus (Acts 18).

(ii) Later, perhaps many years later, he sends the letter mentioned in I Cor. 5.9, from Ephesus.

(iii) Later he receives bad news of the Corinthian Christians from Chloe's household, and Timothy is despatched from Ephesus for Macedonia and Corinth (I Cor. 1.11; 4.17; 16.10; II Cor. 1.1; Acts 19.22).

(iv) I Corinthians is written (possibly in reply to a letter from the Corinthians, I Cor. 7.1) probably near Easter. The Collection for the Christians of Jerusalem is now being organized (I Cor. 16.1; II Cor. 8.6; 12.18).

(v) St. Paul hears of new difficulties in the Corinthian church, especially questioning of his authority; he pays a short visit to Corinth during which he is grossly insulted (II Cor. 2.1; 12.14; 13.1). He returns to Ephesus.

(vi) He sends the 'Severe Letter' (II Cor. 10-13) by Titus from Ephesus to Corinth, with instructions to speed up the Collection for Jerusalem and to return via Macedonia (II Cor. 2.3, 9, 12, 13; 7.5, 6, 8-12).

(vii) He leaves Ephesus (perhaps after the incident of Acts 19.21-41) for Troas, and then, in great anxiety, goes to Macedonia, looking for Titus (II Cor. 2.12, 13).

(viii) He meets Titus in Macedonia and is told encouraging news of the Corinthians; they have undergone a change of heart and the crisis is over (II Cor. 7.6-16). He writes the letter II Cor. 1-9 and sends it from Macedonia[1] by Titus and two brethren (II Cor. 8.16-24).

[1] Possibly from Philippi, as suggested by the subscription to II Corinthians in some manuscripts.

(ix) He reaches Corinth during a stay of three months in Greece, and there he writes the Epistle to the Romans (Acts 19.21; 20.3).

St. Paul would thus have paid three visits to Corinth and have written at least four letters to the Corinthians, of which we have the whole of two, most of another and a small fragment of the fourth.

TRANSLATIONS, COMMENTARIES, ETC.

The Second Epistle to the Corinthians is one of the most difficult books in the New Testament to translate satisfactorily, because its allusions and its language are so obscure. The first half is difficult enough, but the second half, written as it is under the stress of anxiety and indignation, taxes the translator's powers even more severely. Tact in the first half and irony in the second give a peculiar uncertainty to St. Paul's expressions; a literal translation often produces a phrase which is quite meaningless in English, and paraphrase runs the risk of inaccuracy. It is not surprising, then, that the Authorized Version is not at its best in this book, because its compilers, when faced with a very obscure sentence in Greek, usually chose to translate it literally and to let the English meaning look after itself. The Revised Version is a much better translation, but is in this book inevitably inhibited by being a revision of the Authorized Version and not a fresh translation. Moffatt's translation has the virtue of being a completely new one, but is almost too adventurous in its renderings. The translation we recommend most strongly (for this book as for any book of the Bible) is the American Revised Standard Version, which manages to combine the dignity of the older and the accuracy and freshness of the newer Versions in a remarkable way. It has, however, been thought best to base this Commentary upon the text of the Authorized Version (referred to throughout as A.V., just as the Revised Version is referred to as R.V.), though the other translations have been freely quoted.

The standard Commentaries on II Corinthians in English are that by A. Plummer, in the *International Critical Commentary* series (very full, based on the Greek text, abounding in information and indispensable for a scholarly study); that by H. L. Goudge in the *Westminster Commentary* series (full of sound scholarship also, but based on the A.V.); and that by R. H. Strachan in the *Moffatt New Testament Commentary* series (based on Moffatt's translation, and particularly good in sketching the contemporary background to Paul's life and thought). Of these the first and third take the view of the sources of II Corinthians which is taken in this Commentary, but the second defends the older and more conservative view.[1] The book is dealt with more briefly in the pages devoted to it in J. Moffatt's *Introduction to the Literature of the New Testament*. R. V. G. Tasker's *II Corinthians* in the Tyndale New Testament Commentaries, which takes a conservative view on the question of the integrity of the epistle, has appeared since the first edition of this book. A book by a Danish Scholar, J. Munck, called *Paul and the Salvation of Mankind* deals in chapter 6 with II Corinthians and he too is averse to the theory which divides the epistle into two or three. On the nature and function of the apostles two important books have recently appeared, *The Apostolic Succession* by A. Ehrhardt and *The Pioneer Ministry* by A. T. Hanson.

Books dealing with the general background of the New Testament are T. R. Glover's *The World of the New Testament;* H. G. G. Herklots' *A Fresh Approach to the New*

---

[1] In addition to these I have occasionally consulted *Die Briefe an die Korinther*, by Heinz-Dietrich Wendland (Vol. 7 in Das Neue Testament, Deutsch, Göttingen, 1948), and articles in the *Theologisches Wörterbuch zum Neuen Testament*, edited by G. Kittel.

Testament; F. V. Filson's *The New Testament against its Environment,* and also *The Living World of the New Testament,* by H. C. Kee and F. W. Young. Those who want to study St. Paul's Life and Thought should read *The Common Life in the Body of Christ* by L. S. Thornton and *Chapters in a Life of Paul,* by J. Knox (both of which are first class, but neither classifiable as easy reading). A more popular but very useful book is W. Barclay's *The Mind of St. Paul.* A. D. Nock's work on St. Paul in the Home University Library could also be consulted. It would be helpful to look up some of the leading words in this epistle, such as *grace* and *church,* in the *Theological Word Book of the Bible,* edited by Alan Richardson, and to consult the same writer's *Introduction to the Theology of the New Testament.*

I

THE MAIN LETTER
1.1–6.13; 7.2–9.15; 13.11-14

THE GREETING
1.1-2

1. an apostle of Jesus Christ by the will of God

Notice that St. Paul describes himself thus, whereas he only describes Timothy as OUR BROTHER, obviously making a distinction. What exactly Paul meant by calling himself an apostle will be considered later on (see Note on pp. 59-64).

the church of God which is at Corinth

Does not mean all people in Corinth who happen to be interested in Christianity, nor does it mean an outlying sub-division of a great organization whose Headquarters are at Jerusalem or Rome. To Paul the Church at Corinth is neither a voluntary society (e.g. the bird-watchers of Corinth) nor a section of a centralized organization (e.g. the Christian Co-operative Society, Corinth Subdivision, No. 1), but something vaster and more unified than the first and more independent and fully representative than the second. THE CHURCH OF GOD WHICH IS AT CORINTH means members of the redeemed society, the corporate instrument of God's redeeming and healing activity in the world, the Christian international in Corinth, the manifestation of the Body of Christ in Corinth. But in these Christians the whole Church was fully represented; when they met together the whole Christ was fully with them; when they prayed the whole Church prayed with them. This is one of the ways in which the sharing of life and experience in Christ, which Paul assumes to be the possession of all Christians, manifests itself. The Corinthian church is only part of a whole, and yet the whole is there.

saints

Does not of course mean people of what we should now call saintly lives (the rest of II Corinthians should make this unmistakably clear!), but people who have received God's calling in Christ to separate themselves from the world for his saving purposes. Compare 'called to be saints' in Rom. 1.7.

Achaia

Was the name of a province of the Roman Empire corresponding roughly to the southern half of the modern Kingdom of Greece; it would not include Thessalonica or Beroea or Philippi. It was at the time St. Paul wrote governed by a pro-consul who was responsible directly to the Senate and not to the Roman Emperor.

2. Grace . . . and peace

These are words which we take very much for granted to-day, but for these Corinthians they must have had new and amazing associations, because they believed themselves to be living in a New Order determined by a new relationship to God which they called by these names, GRACE AND PEACE (for a fuller note on grace, see below, p. 67).

THE INTERCHANGE IN CHRIST
1.3-14

These verses expound as no others in all St. Paul's writings the interchange of opposite experiences which is the privilege of those who are in Christ. This is the particular form taken in this Epistle by the thanksgiving for the faith of those to whom he is writing which regularly appears in every

authentic letter of St. Paul (with the significant exception of
Galatians). A special note on this subject is attached to
the end of this section of the Commentary.

6. the enduring of the same sufferings which we also suffer:
What were these sufferings, and what, indeed, is the meaning of the whole verse? It is possible that Paul's sufferings
were simply his intense disgust at the behaviour of the
Corinthians which reduced him almost to his death-bed
(vv. 9, 10), in which case his suffering would be for the
Corinthians' salvation because it induced in him a painful
but wholesome severity, and his comfort would console them
because it would mean that he now approved of their conduct. But though he speaks in 7.5 of his extreme wretched-
ness of mind induced by their misconduct, this was in
Macedonia, and not in Asia. Moreover the WHETHER WE BE
AFFLICTED of v. 6 seems to be echoed in the TROUBLE of v. 8
which came upon Paul (R.V. translates 'afflicted' and
'affliction', because the words have the same root in Greek)
when he was in Asia, and this affliction does not seem to
have originated from the Corinthians, especially as Paul believes himself to have been helped out of it by the Corinthians' prayers (v. 11). It is better therefore to assume that
the affliction referred to in vv. 6 and 8 is some grave danger
that befell him while he was in Ephesus, not long before he
set out to Macedonia to meet Titus, some serious illness, or
perhaps an imprisonment (cf. I Cor. 15.32).

9. we had the sentence of death in ourselves
This is ambiguous; R.V. has 'answer of death'. The
Greek word (*apokrima*) cannot mean an opinion or sentiment, so that the words cannot mean that Paul had con-
cluded that he was destined to death. Originally *apokrima*
means an official answer given after enquiry. Probably Paul
means that in this grave peril he felt like a prisoner who had
asked for mercy and had received the answer that he must
die.

12. 'For our boast is this, the testimony of our conscience that we have behaved in the world, and still more toward you, with holiness and godly sincerity. . . .' (Revised Standard.)

13. For we write none other things unto you than what ye read and acknowledge

It is difficult at first to see the point of this; what else could Paul write to the Corinthians except what they read? Plummer (in the *International Critical Commentary*, p. 26) takes it to mean that Paul is defending himself against the charge of writing ambiguous and deliberately obscure letters, for the Corinthian Church would by now have had at least three letters from him. But this seems a rather odd accusation for the Corinthians to make, quite apart from the fact that it would mean that Paul had answered it by writing a letter which is obscurer and more ambiguous than any of his other surviving ones. There is a play on words in the Greek here, impossible to reproduce in English; the same Greek word without a preposition or compounded with different prepositions can mean 'know', 'read' or 'recognize'. So Paul probably means: 'I write nothing except what you read in your formal assembly and acknowledge as authoritative.' And he hopes that they will continue acknowledging his letters as authoritative indefinitely (TO THE END).

14. ye have acknowledged us in part

A party in Corinth still withholds full recognition from Paul. The phrase could be translated: 'you have known us in part' (as all the occurrences of 'acknowledge' in these verses could be translated 'know'); but this produces a less precise and less relevant meaning in the context; cf. 2.5.

in the day of the Lord Jesus

The Day with a capital D, the day when Jesus will come to judge, which Paul conceived as coming very soon (cf. Rom. 2.5-16; 13.11, 12; I Cor. 3.11-15; 4.5; II Cor. 5.10;

II Thess. 1.5-10). He can use the present tense because as
far as Paul's claim on the Corinthians and theirs on him are
concerned the Day has taken place; they are Christ's now,
and so they are each other's; cf. I Cor. 3.21-23. The Day,
when it comes, will not alter this; it will only make it unmistakably clear.

NOTE ON INTERCHANGE OF EXPERIENCE IN CHRIST

'For as the sufferings of Christ abound in us, so our con-
solation also aboundeth by Christ,' says St. Paul, and the
whole passage, 1.1-7, elaborates the meaning of this strange
claim. Indeed this passage is only the first of a series of
similar ones making in effect very much the same claim:
that is, that the man who is in Christ shares in his own
person the same paradox, the same divinely ordained contradiction, as that which the life and destiny of Jesus Christ
constituted, the paradox of comfort from suffering, of life
from death, of strength from weakness, of wisdom from
foolishness. To Paul the Crucifixion of Jesus Christ was
the paradox *par excellence*, the greatest turning of the tables,
the vastest confounding of human expectation of all time.
Out of the suffering, the death, the helplessness and what
appeared to be the folly of Jesus had come from God comfort, life, strength and wisdom. This meant that because
Christians do not merely imitate, follow or feel inspired by
Christ, but actually live in him, are part of him, dwell
supernaturally in a new world where the air they breathe is
his Spirit, then for them henceforward suffering accepted
in Christ must bring comfort, death accepted in Christ must
bring life, weakness accepted in Christ must bring strength
and foolishness accepted in Christ must bring wisdom.
There is for the Christian an interchange between these
opposites, a divine transforming of each into the other.

But this is true for Paul not only of the individual in his
personal relation to Christ, but also of the relations of

Christians to each other. If we look at three of the passages in II Corinthians where Paul refers to this Interchange, we can see this plainly. The first is 1.1-7, where it is plain that suffering in one Christian (Paul) becomes comfort in another, in this case a group of Christians (the Corinthians). Because the Corinthians share Christ with Paul, they also share Paul's sufferings in Christ, and, as a necessary consequence, Paul's comfort. The next passage is 4.8-12, where it is explicitly stated that death, working in Christ's apostle Paul, becomes life in the Corinthians. And there is a series of passages in the second half of this work which draw out the interchange of weakness and strength for those who are in Christ—11.30; 12.5, 8-10, and finally the passage which ends with the magnificent statement (13.2-9), 'I will not spare: Since ye seek a proof of Christ speaking in me, which to you-ward is not weak, but is mighty in you. For though he was crucified through weakness, yet he liveth by the power of God. For we also are weak in him, but we shall live with him by the power of God toward you.' Weakness in Paul can become strength in the Corinthians; it can become strength in Paul too, for all Christians have in themselves both weakness and strength, both suffering and comfort, both life and death, both foolishness and wisdom, as sharing in the life of the One who embodied in himself and his life and death and resurrection all these paradoxes. And Christians share with each other this interchange of experience. The mystery of Christ's Interchange flows over from him to them and also from each of them to the others. The Interchange of foolishness and wisdom is described in I Corinthians 1.18-31, and Paul's thought elsewhere in his letters is deeply influenced by this conviction, though nowhere so much as in II Corinthians (cf. Rom. 15.1-7; I Cor. 4.9, 10; Phil. 2.5-11; and also II Cor. 7.5-7).

Two consequences seem to follow from this remarkable conviction. The first is that its attitude to suffering is one of the strong points of Christianity. Simone Weil, the French girl of Jewish race whose writings are now attract-

ing so much interest, observed that the great strength of
Christianity lay in the fact that it did not profess to cure
suffering, but it did profess to use it. The problem of suffering is one which every religion has somehow to face. Christianity faces it by making suffering the means by which
healing and rescue were brought to the world, and the
very stock-in-trade and accustomed diet of Christians. Yet
to Christians suffering is not a deliberately contrived
instrument for atonement as it is to the Indian fanatic who
tortures himself in order to gain the peace of detachment,
but an evil force in the world which yet by Christ's atonement can be used for redemption and healing, even in the
individual's personal life.

The other consequence is that if the Church accepts this
Interchange as part of her life, she can never become wholly
satisfied with her situation in the world. In the past the
Church has often fallen to the temptation of becoming quite
satisfied with her position in society, her status and achievement and privileges, and has succeeded almost in driving
deliberately accepted suffering out of her life. We can think
of the Church of Laodicea which said, 'I am rich, and in-
creased with goods, and have need of nothing', and did not
know that it was 'wretched, and miserable, and poor, and
blind, and naked' (Rev. 3.17); or we can recall the bloated
stagnation of the Mediaeval Church against which St.
Francis protested, or the bourgeois complacency of the
'Barchester' type of church life in the last century, and of
many rather similar types in this century. Patterns of church
life such as these had succeeded in squeezing out the suffering of Christ from their fabric, and were thus far unfaithful
to their calling. Suffering is a part of the normal life of the
Christian Church anywhere at any time, and if the Church
happens to live in a society like ours which tries to run
away from and forget such things as suffering and death
and the tragic dimension of human existence, it becomes the
duty of the Church to stimulate society, and not to soothe
it, to remind men of their need and hunger and wretched-

ness, and of their involvement in the suffering of the world, and not to assure them that they are very decent citizens and good fellows who only lack a spiritual background for their lives.

WHY PAUL WROTE INSTEAD OF PAYING
A VISIT
1.15–2.17

15. a second benefit

Here the R.V. Margin tells us that an alternative translation is ' grace ' and that some ancient authorities read a word instead which means ' joy '.   Plummer, *International Critical Commentary*, p. 32, and the Revised Standard Version prefer the reading ' joy '; it is impossible to decide finally between them.   How this visit would have conferred A SECOND BENEFIT is uncertain; it is most probable that Paul had already visited them twice, once for his first, evangelizing, visit and once for his short and painful one (see above, Introduction p. 13 and note on 12.14, p. 89). Perhaps he means ' a second happy visit ', not counting his painful visit as a benefit or joy.

17. did I use lightness?

The R.V. translation ' did I shew fickleness? ' is better, and the Revised Standard: ' was I vacillating? ' is better still.   St. Paul had decided to pay them a visit but changed his mind when, half-way there (beyond Troas, 2.12, 13), he met Titus (7.6) and learnt of their change of heart and behaviour (7.7).

according to the flesh

Means ' according to merely human standards and judgments' (see the note on pp. 48-9).

that with me there should be yea yea, and nay nay?

This does *not* mean ' that with me my Yes should

C

be Yes and my No No' but precisely the opposite.
The Revised Standard Version translates: 'Do I make
my plans like a worldly man, ready to say Yes and No
at once?'

19-22. Everything that was promised or declared by God
in the Old Testament finds its fulfilment in Christ. Christ is
the guarantee that when God promises he is faithful to
his promise, the proof that God's promises were true
promises. And consequently Christ is the Person in whom
we can say Amen to God. He is the place where humanity
makes its free and loving response to what God has done for
it. It was evidently the custom in Christian worship for even
the humblest and least educated worshipper to say Amen
at the end of other people's utterances (I Cor. 14.16). Christ
is called 'the Amen, the faithful and true witness' in Rev.
3.14; and in Rev. 7.12 the angels fall on their faces before
the throne and say, 'Amen: Blessing, and glory, and wisdom, and thanksgiving, and honour, and power, and might,
be unto our God for ever and ever. Amen.' Even in so
small a point as this the mediatorial position which the
early Church gave to Jesus is evident; he is God's pledge
of his faithfulness to men, and men's expression of their
faith in God. It is from this conviction, that God has in
Christ moved out to us and that we in Christ return to him
in worship, that the Christian doctrine of the Trinity ultim-
ately springs. Only in the Spirit (v. 22), through the Son,
can we return to the God who has moved out to us in his
Son.

21-22. Though it would be quite wrong to see in this passage
a reference to Confirmation (there is no clear and indisput-
able evidence that Christians as early as this were anointed
with oil or had hands laid on them as part of Christian initia-
tion), the tenses of the Greek verbs and the association of
baptism with the Spirit throughout the New Testament make
it very likely that St. Paul conceived that this establishing,

anointing, sealing, and giving of the EARNEST OF THE SPIRIT
took place for Christians at their baptism. Christians were
anointed because they had received the Spirit, with whom
the Messiah (the Anointed One) was anointed (Isa. 44.1-5;
61.1-3; Mark 1.9-12). Sealing implied security against viola-
tion, and also a guarantee of genuineness, and is used often
in the Bible literally and metaphorically (I Kings 21.8; Dan.
6.17; Matt. 27.66; Deut. 32.34; Job 14.17; 37.7; Isa. 8.16;
John 3.33; 6.27; Eph. 1.13; 4.30), and particularly in the
book of the Revelation (7.3-8; 10.4; 20.3; 22.10). A Christian was sealed because he was set aside by God as God's
special property, was inviolable by the devil and had God's
guarantee of his salvation.

earnest
   Means 'first instalment'. The Christian possessed in the
Spirit a first instalment of Heaven; cf. Eph. 1.14. We shall
recur to this thought in the fifth chapter (see pp. 43-4).

23. upon my soul
   This is how A.V. and R.V. translate. Moffatt and Revised
Standard render it: 'against my soul'.

2.1-13. St. Paul explains that the effect of the 'Severe Letter'
sent by Titus brought about such a change of opinion among
the Corinthians against the man who was causing him most
trouble that he found it unnecessary to visit them, and even
begs them not to be too hard on the offender. But he is
anxious to make it clear that he has been greatly troubled
by their conduct.

2. It is, says St. Paul, against my interests to pain you, for
I deprive myself of my sole source of pleasure by doing so.

5. The A.V. translation is definitely wrong here. Follow
the R.V. and the Revised Standard, which last runs: 'But
if any one has caused pain, he has caused it not to me, but

in some measure—not to put it too severely—to you all.'

12, 13. when I came to Troas to preach Christ's gospel,
even though **a door was opened unto me of the Lord, I had
no rest in my spirit.**

14-16. Paul as a preacher of the Gospel is like a sweet smell
going up to Heaven. Two pictures probably unite here:
(i) the picture of a Roman general on his triumphal proces-
sion through the capital (CAUSETH US TO TRIUMPH, 14), when
incense would be burnt by bystanders all along the way;
(ii) the picture of the burning of the fat in a sacrifice to God
(cf. Gen. 8.20, 21; Ex. 29.18; Ezek. 20.41; Mal. 3.4; Phil.
4.18; Eph. 5.2). In both pictures the thought is that Paul's
work is something given for God's glory and done in Christ.
But Paul points out the double-edged nature of such work.
The sweet smell can be a SAVOUR either OF DEATH UNTO
DEATH or OF LIFE UNTO LIFE (16). This is a characteristic
that attaches to all God's gifts (because the preaching of the
gospel, while it is a work done for God, is also from the
point of view of the hearer, a gift, a work done by God; it
is done in Christ the Mediator). God's privileges are always
also responsibilities; God's grace is also God's judgment.
God always meets man as an undeserved gift, but the gift
forces the recipient to choose, either for death or for life.
Cf. I Cor. 11.26-32.

THE ETERNAL AND THE TEMPORARY IN
THE CHRISTIAN'S RELATION TO
GOD IN CHRIST
3.1.–6.10

DIVINE LIGHT
3.1–4.6

Having explained carefully his reasons for not visiting the
Corinthians, St. Paul now observes, without in the least hurt-

ing the feelings of his hearers, that he really has no need to
make such explanations, because his relation to them and
their relation to God in Christ are such that they should
accept him without criticism as the divinely appointed minister of God's New Light to them. In order to emphasize
this point Paul, most fortunately for us, thought it right to
give an account, unequalled in the sweep and richness of
its thought, of how this New Light reaches his converts
through an apostle.

He begins by using two different images from the Old
Testament. The first (3.1-6) is that of the Law written on
the heart, where he mingles both the words of Jeremiah
about God writing his law in the inward parts of his people,
and those of Ezekiel about God giving his people hearts of
flesh instead of hearts of stone, and contrasts these inscribed
hearts, so to speak, with the inscribed tablets of Moses' Law
(Jer. 31.33; Ezek. 11.19; 36.26; Ex. 31.18). This blending
of Old Testament images and passages is highly characteristic of St. Paul. It serves, in this instance, to bring out the
contrast between the Law contained in ordinances regulat-
ing behaviour and externally imposed, of the old covenant,
and the knowledge of God's will through the indwelling
Spirit open to every man who is in Christ, under the new
covenant. The relation between apostle and converts, Paul
implies, should be a reflection of the relation between Christ
and the Christian, one of entire trust, grounded upon new
light, new revelation.

The second image which St. Paul uses (3.7–4.6) is taken
from the story in Exodus (34.29-35) relating how Moses
found it necessary to put a veil on his face when he came
near to the people of Israel immediately after he had been
communing with God (presumably at the Tabernacle).
Moses, says St. Paul, was in this a type, a foreshadowing, a
divinely ordained dress rehearsal, so to speak, of Christ, and
also of Christ's minister, the apostle. Just as the people of
Israel could have seen God's light reflected in Moses' face,
but for the veil, so Christians to-day, possessing the Spirit,

see God's light reflected in Christ, and the apostle ministers
God's light to his converts. But Paul, who can hardly ever
leave an Old Testament image alone without blending it
with something else, sees Moses' significance in this story as
twofold. He represents Christ and Christ's minister, but he
also represents the Law and everything in the Jewish religion
which was hindering Christianity. As reflecting God's light,
he is a type of the Law, that collection of written commandments the keeping of which represented to the pious Jew
God's last word about the way to please him, and which, as
Paul realized so clearly, must be regarded by Christians as
only God's second-last word, superseded by his last Word
spoken in Christ. So he describes Moses as a minister of
THE LETTER which KILLETH and speaks of the ministration
of death, WRITTEN AND ENGRAVEN IN STONES (picking up
again his first Old Testament image), of the GLORY which
WAS TO BE DONE AWAY of the MINISTRATION OF CONDEMNA-
TION and of THAT WHICH IS DONE AWAY (vv. 6, 7, 9, 11).

This double role which Paul assigns to Moses in fact
reflects his view of the function of the Law in God's plan for
mankind. To Paul, the Law is both good and holy, as
ordained by God and pointing on to Christ, and also in-
effective and temporary, as superseded by Christ; and in
the Law (i.e. the Pentateuch primarily, but the word is capable also in Paul's thought of including the rest of the Old
Testament), he believes that we can find evidence that
Moses not only gave Israel a law of commandments to live
by as a temporary dispensation, but also spoke and wrote
about the coming of the new, permanent dispensation in
Christ (see Rom. 10.4-19; I Cor. 10.1-4). To St. Paul, indeed, Moses virtually *is* the Law; he almost is the Law
incarnate, and not least in this passage in II Corinthians (a
similar double role is played in St. Paul's thought by Adam
who is the type both of the primal sin and of the 'life-giving
spirit' who was to come).

And indeed without necessarily committing ourselves to
St. Paul's characteristically Rabbinic treatment of the Old

Testament, we may well agree that there is a genuine truth behind his contrast between the Law inscribed-on-tablets of the old covenant and the law-written-on-hearts-by-the-Spirit of the new, and behind the two roles which he conceives Moses as playing. It is the contrast between imagining that the will of God is conceived and codified in a number of commandments, numerous or few, important or trivial, and that pleasing God consists in keeping these; and imagining that the will of God is revealed in a Person, and that pleasing God consists in being united to that Person and living in his life. It is, in fact, the contrast between Christianity on the one hand and on the other any religion which teaches that God's will can be known by a code of morals or standard of behaviour in which that will has been, so to speak, registered. Christianity therefore is here contrasted no less with the average Englishman's idea of Christianity as decency and tolerance and fair play and the American's idea of Christianity as consisting primarily of the Sermon on the Mount, than it is with the religion of the Old Testament.

1. again
Here surely refers to the ' Severe Letter '; and there can be no doubt that in II Cor. 10-13 St. Paul was concerned to commend himself!

10. had no glory in this respect, by reason of the glory that excelleth is a literal translation of the Greek, but this is obviously not intelligible English. IN THIS RESPECT BY REASON OF is a rather clumsy way of saying ' compared with '. We might paraphrase the whole verse thus: ' But because of the transcendent glory that which had been glorified lost its glory in comparison.'

13. Every recent commentator takes END here to mean ' full stop ', and many are puzzled to know why Moses in Paul's conception should want to prevent the people of Israel see-

ing that the glory on his face was destined to end. In fact it
is much more satisfactory to take END here as meaning:
' ordained fulfilment '.[1] What St. Paul means is that Moses
put the veil on to prevent the Jews perceiving what was the
fulfilment of that which was being done away. And to-day,
he adds, when the Scriptures are read, the Jews, because
of this veil, fail to see that the fulfilment of what they see
is Christ (it is not merely that they fail to see that the Mosaic
dispensation is temporary). But why should Paul apparently
say that Moses deliberately put on this veil? Two reasons
suggest themselves for this: first, that in the account in
Exodus Moses did in fact put on the veil in order to prevent the Jews seeing his face, at their request; and secondly,
that Paul (whose mind was of a thoroughly Hebraic cast) is
always inclined to see the hand of God in any human
activity, even in the activity of those who run away from
God. The Jews of old would not look at Moses, and the Jews
to-day will not realize when Moses' works are read that they
speak of Christ. This is their own fault certainly (for THE
GOD OF THIS WORLD HATH BLINDED their MINDS, 4.4); but it
is also ordained and designed by God for his own purposes
(see Rom. 9-11, where St. Paul deals with exactly the same
subject at much greater length).

16, 17. It is possible that Paul thought that wherever the
Old Testament referred to the LORD it meant Christ; certainly he believed that it was Christ whom Moses saw when
he saw the LORD in the Tabernacle. But Christ *is* the Spirit
(St. Paul does not seem to distinguish the two here; cf. Rom.
8.26, 27, 34), and the Spirit gives the true interpretation of
the Old Testament. NOW THE LORD IS THAT SPIRIT may
mean ' Now, the Lord in this passage means the Spirit '.
To St. Paul Moses' turning to the Spirit was equivalent to
his turning to Christ.

[1] It is this passage, with Rom. 10.4, that convinces me that it is unjusti-
fiable to confine the New Testament meanings of *telos* to mean ' full
stop '. Contemporary secular usage certainly did not so confine them.

18. beholding as in a glass the glory of the Lord

Most modern commentators prefer the alternative rendering of the R.V.: 'reflecting as a mirror' (and so, in effect, Moffatt). The uses of the word in literature outside the New Testament could give either meaning. In view, however, of the fact that the interpretation of the Old Testament has been so much in Paul's mind, it is more satisfactory to keep the A.V. reading BEHOLDING AS IN A GLASS, and I Cor. 13.12 supports this ('For now we see through a glass darkly, but then face to face'). Because Christians have the Spirit, they can behold the glory of God where Jews cannot behold it (though even they see only a reflection; the full view, 'face to face', is reserved for the next life), and they are consequently changed by their beholding.

from glory to glory, possibly 'moving from one stage of glory to another' or (Revised Standard) 'from one degree of glory to another'; but more probably 'from glory gaining glory', i.e. from beholding Christ's glory reaching the point of reflecting his glory ourselves.

4.1-6. He moves now from Ex. 34 to Gen. 1.3 ('And God said, Let there be light, and there was light'), a clearer and grander background for his doctrine of divine light.

3, 4. Salvation is at the same time ruin for those who will not hear (see the note on 2.14-16, p. 36). St. Paul does not believe that God will continue indefinitely to offer salvation to those who refuse to listen. Indeed the whole conviction, so evident everywhere in the New Testament, that the coming of Jesus constitutes a crisis of the greatest imaginable urgency precludes this belief.

6. In Christ God has brought about a new creation (cf. 5.17 and Gal. 6.15). St. Paul does not mean this as a mere figure of speech, but literally. Christianity is not just a new set of ideas, nor a new way of life, nor a new morality, but a new Person; and to be united to that Person, to live in his life (not simply to follow his example nor to be inspired by his ideals, but supernaturally to be brought into the life of his Body by Baptism and to continue in that life through faith) was in truth and in fact to take part in an existence, a universe, newly brought into being for men by God. In order to deal with evil and its effects,[1] which put into the hands of men something not unlike the power to create something new and without parallel in the world of nature, God brought about in his Son a new creation, a new order of existence, existence in Christ. Christians therefore are inevitably people who live in two worlds, two orders, the unredeemed and the redeemed. And it is to the tension between these two that St. Paul next turns.

HUMAN LIMITATIONS
4.7–6.10

From the consideration of the greatness of the Christian's privilege in possessing this new light, Paul turns to face the fact that even those who have this light have to live in mortal bodies and in a sinful world, and to the clearer defining of his status as an apostle called to minister this light.

7-18. The Interchange of Suffering and Comfort in Christ of the first chapter becomes here the Interchange of Life and Death in Christ (see the Note, pp. 30-3).

13. I believed, and therefore have I spoken
This is a quotation from Ps. 116.10, and it is possible, indeed likely, that St. Paul thought that it was Christ who through the Spirit spoke in the Psalm; hence the words WE HAVING THE SAME SPIRIT in this verse.

15. The R.V. translation is preferable here: 'that the grace,

[1] Moral evil: we are not here concerned with pain and physical imperfection.

being multiplied through the many, may cause the thanksgiving to abound ' (cf. 1.11).

4.16-5.10. In order to explain his power of continuing to minister divine light in spite of human limitations, St. Paul now spends a few sentences on considering the destiny of our bodies, and of our whole personalities in the future, and incidentally provides one of the fullest (and most obscure) passages on the subject of the Resurrection of the body in the New Testament.[1]   There are several points which we must remember in reading this passage :

(i) St. Paul, like all Christians of his time, apparently believed that what we call the Second Coming, but what he called the Arrival (*Parousia*) of Christ was going to take place very soon, probably in his lifetime. He was therefore not interested in the question which is probably the one that would interest us most in considering the life to come, What happens to me when I die?, because he believed that probably he would not have to undergo physical death as we know it, or if he did have to, he would only be dead for a very short time before the Resurrection (he would not of course say ' dead ', but ' departed with Christ ', Phil. 1.23; or ' asleep ', I Cor. 15.6, and I Thess. 4.15; or possibly I Thess. 4.16, ' dead in Christ ').

(ii) The words WORKETH FOR US A FAR MORE EXCEEDING AND ETERNAL WEIGHT OF GLORY (4.17) and HE THAT HATH WROUGHT US FOR THE SELF-SAME THING refer to the same conviction, that God is recreating us in Christ (see the note on 4.6, pp. 41-2). The pledge, guarantee and *first instalment* of this (EARNEST 5.5) is the possession of the Spirit given through Baptism. In a sense therefore this passage is only elaborating the statement already made that God has brought about a new creation in Christ. Like the process

---

[1] The relation of this with the other long passage in St. Paul's Letters, I Cor. 15, is very well dealt with in L. S. Thornton's *The Common Life in the Body of Christ*, Part II, Ch. ix, pp. 284-5.

of the first creation (as we now know it from the discoveries of science) this new creation is a long process, inaugurated at Baptism for each of us, but not completed till the General Resurrection.

(iii) This process of re-creation transforms us from being spirits weighed down by earthly perishable bodies to being spirits glorified by supernatural bodies. The supernatural Spirit at work in us initiates this redemption, but it is finally accomplished at the Arrival of Christ, at which point our physical bodies will be transformed into spiritual bodies. To St. Paul a bodiless existence is not the natural destiny of human personalities; they may have to undergo such an existence for a period of waiting before the Arrival, but this is not their complete and final state.[1] The human personality needs a body for its full expression, but when God finally orders the universe wholly according to his will the bodies which human beings will possess will not be their present physical bodies; these Paul consistently regards as perishable and incapable of meeting the demands of existence in glory (the WEIGHT OF GLORY, 4.17; cf. I Cor. 15.50, ' flesh and blood cannot inherit the Kingdom of God '). This alone should suffice to distinguish true Christian piety towards the dead and hope for the dead from the sub-Christian preoccupation with the grave, the coffin, the funeral monument and the trappings of burial which often today when deaths occur tend to replace genuine Christian faith and hope. Both science and theology agree that into the grave is placed no more than the perishable shell or envelope of the human being who, if he survives at all, does not survive there. The process of transformation from personality-involved-in-perishable-body to personality-glorified-by-spiritual-body St. Paul in this passage describes in the grand words, THAT MORTALITY MIGHT BE SWALLOWED UP OF LIFE. (In I Cor. 15.35-53 he gives a much fuller description of the same process).

[1] See the Note on Body and Soul in St. Paul's thought at the end of the Section (pp. 53-7).

(iv) St. Paul expressly tells us that in this passage he is thinking only of those who will be alive at the Arrival when he uses the words IF SO BE THAT BEING CLOTHED WE SHALL NOT BE FOUND NAKED (5.3). We might indeed paraphrase this and the preceding verse thus: 'Because in this body we groan, desiring to put on our building which is from heaven, assuming, that is, that when we do put it on we shall not be in a state of bodilessness' (that is, assuming that when the time of putting on the spiritual body comes we shall not have departed this life). It is probable that the expression translated by the A.V. IF SO BE THAT and paraphrased above 'assuming, that is, that', implies an uncertainty in Paul's mind as to whether he can with confidence assume that he will still be alive when the Arrival takes place (cf. 'if it be in vain' or 'assuming that it is in vain' of Gal. 3.4). This would mean that St. Paul was not ignoring the situation of the person who has died before the Arrival (he does not do so in I Cor. 15 nor I Thess. 4), but just not concentrating particularly on it here.

(v) Does St. Paul imply that the spiritual body, which is what he means by A BUILDING OF GOD, AN HOUSE NOT MADE WITH HANDS, ETERNAL, is *already* waiting for us in the heavens? His language certainly makes it difficult for us to rule out this conclusion. In some sense the spiritual body is already prepared for us by God. Indeed it is quite possible that the words of v. 3, IF SO BE THAT BEING CLOTHED WE SHALL NOT BE FOUND NAKED, may not refer at all to the possibility of Paul's having departed this life by the time the Resurrection takes place, but to the possibility that he will not have deserved it (cf. Rev. 3.4; 6.11; 7.9, where the white robes are probably the spiritual body given to the martyrs as their reward), and that we are to think of the spiritual body as something that we can gradually grow into, so to speak, even in this life (for Paul's fears lest he may not achieve final salvation cf. I Cor. 9.26-7; Phil. 3.10-14). If this is a possible interpretation, it would largely remove the difficulty of conceiving how a perishable body can after it

has wholly decayed and perhaps disappeared be transformed
into a spiritual body.   The human being would on this
assumption (which is not incompatible with the seed-flower
analogy of I Cor. 15) leave the physical body finally at or
soon after physical death, but would still retain, and perhaps
have opportunities of increasing, his connection with the
spiritual body, which he would not however fully enjoy
until the General Resurrection.   In any case, Paul certainly
sees the Spirit as the sure and unbreakable link between
our present existence in perishable bodies and our future
existence in spiritual bodies.

We should not, it must be remembered, make too absolute
a division in our minds between this age, this life, this order,
and the next, because in the minds of the people who wrote
the New Testament the two ages and orders overlapped.
Indeed it was in the Spirit that they overlapped.   This is the
whole point of St. Paul's doctrine of the Last Things.   In
so far as we are in the Spirit, we are almost emancipated
from moral law.   We can *almost* say ' All things are lawful
to me ' (I Cor. 6.12; 10.23).   We are risen, we are liberated,
and yet—not quite.   Sin and death, temptation and disease,
have still to be fought in our body, or, as St. Paul would say,
' mortified ' (Rom. 8.13; Col. 3.5).   The decisive battle
against these evil things has been won by Christ on the Cross
(Col. 2.8-15), but the ' mopping-up operations ' have yet to
be undertaken by Christ in his members, the Christians,
before the campaign is completely finished, the end unmistakably reached and God's everlastingly successful reconstruction accomplished.   From time to time during Christian
history groups of Christians have declared, ' We are redeemed, and need take no more notice of morality.'   But
they have always forgotten that even though we live in the
Spirit we are not completely redeemed before the redemption
of the body.

10. This verse alone should make it clear that Christianity
cannot fairly be accused of teaching its followers to ignore

the inequalities and injustices of this world in order to con-
centrate wholly upon securing their happiness in the next,
nor of preaching a gospel of 'pie in the sky when you die '.
Here St. Paul says unconditionally that your fate in the next
world depends upon what you have done in this world (THE
THINGS DONE IN HIS BODY, ACCORDING TO THAT HE HATH
DONE, WHETHER IT BE GOOD OR BAD).   Christianity certainly
teaches that this world is not the end, is not indeed even the
most important type of existence, and the appalling results of
believing in philosophies, such as Marxism, which hold that
this world *is* the end seem to justify this teaching.   But
Christians are also expected to believe that their behaviour
in this world is entirely crucial for their destiny in the next.
They will get 'pie in the sky' when they die, but not if they
have done their best to monopolize pie for themselves while
they were in the body.   With this passage compare I Cor.
3.12-15, where the same thing is said even more emphatically,
and Rom. 14.10.   All through the New Testament, in fact,
there runs the conviction that though the judgment in the
sense of sentence, not verdict, will only be passed on each
man on the Last Day, yet it is what each man is doing *now*
that determines, that is determining, the verdict; cf. John
3.16-21.

5.10-6.10. St. Paul again brings the theme back to his own
special position and responsibility as an apostle.   In effect
he says; I am not thinking of my position or yours by purely
human standards, secularly.   I am confident that God
knows my good intentions, and you ought to also.   What
compels me to act as I do is the love of Christ.   I am his
representative, bound and commissioned to declare his
love.

11. The Revised Standard Version is most intelligible:
'Knowing the fear of the Lord, we persuade men, but what
we are is known to God, and I hope it is known also to
your conscience.'

14. If one died for all, then were all dead

The R.V. is better: then all died. It is almost shocking to realize how literally St. Paul takes the fact that we are in Christ, even before we are baptized. Here he is saying, without using metaphor or poetic exaggeration, that when Christ died on the Cross, then all men died in him; in some supernatural sense the whole human race died when Christ died, because the Incarnation meant that he was not only the Representative, but also the incorporated Head of the human race, not merely its leader or finest example, but the personified principle of its existence. What happened to him then in some sense happened to the whole race.

16. What is the meaning of knowing somebody AFTER THE FLESH? Or, a more important question, what is the meaning of knowing Christ AFTER THE FLESH? It has been suggested that this means that St. Paul knew personally the historical Jesus, or that he once held a Judaistic, semi-Christian faith in Jesus. Both of these suggestions are, quite rightly, rejected by most recent commentators. AFTER THE FLESH must mean: secularly, by purely human standards, as WE PERSUADE MEN and IN APPEARANCE in vv. 11 and 12 have already implied. St. Paul is saying here that he no longer regards Christ as simply a figure of history (using 'flesh' in apparently just the same sense as the Fourth Evangelist uses it in John 6.63, 'the flesh profiteth nothing'), just as he does not estimate anybody simply by his worldly or secular worth.

We can see at once that this is in fact the whole difference between the Christian believer and the agnostic to-day. To the agnostic, Jesus is a peculiarly inspired religious leader, or a very pathetic victim of injustice, or an unfortunate fanatic whose impossible views cost him his life. To the believer his life did not end with the Crucifixion, it revived with the Resurrection, and therefore he cannot be classed simply with other figures of history, other great religious leaders. And for the same reason, Jesus cannot and must not be estimated simply by his historical utterances, by the Beatitudes or by the Sermon on the Mount, or by his actions simply on the plane of history, by his attitude towards publicans, harlots and outcasts, or by his cleansing of the Temple. To judge him thus is to judge him AFTER THE FLESH. He is to be judged by the fact that he was 'declared to be the Son of God . . . by the resurrection of the dead' (Rom. 1.4); any other judgment is, from the Christian point of view, meaningless. St. Paul maintains this view consistently throughout his writings, showing very little interest in the ministry of Jesus before its last week, and absolutely none in Jesus as Teacher or as Hero (see also the note on 10.2, p. 74).

17. See note on 4.6 (pp. 41-2). The reality of this new creation is shown by the fact that Christ had to die in order to bring it about and that Christians have to die in Christ in order to take part in it.

18-20. A careful reading of these verses will make it clear that St. Paul undoubtedly sees himself, in his capacity as an apostle, as standing between God and men, and with God's authority bringing the message of reconciliation to them. The 'we's' and the 'you's' of these verses refer respectively to Paul the Apostle and to his Corinthian converts; the 'we' cannot refer to all Christians, otherwise there is no point in introducing the 'you' at all. This function of reconciliation is, further, one which by its nature the apostle must needs pass on to others. This passage is, indeed, one of the charters of the Christian ministry[1] in the New Testament.

18. who hath reconciled us to himself by Jesus Christ
It has often been pointed out that Paul does not say that God reconciled himself to us; God did not have to change

[1] For further consideration of this question, see the note at the end of this section on Apostleship.

D

his attitude to us, but ours to him.   Yet this is only half true,
for two reasons:

(i) In a sense God did change his attitude to us, in the
most drastic and wholehearted way. He moved out to meet
us; in the Person of his Son he emptied himself, he committed, pledged himself. He did not merely remain loving
towards us, he *acted* in love, he committed himself to time
and space, to human existence. This was something new,
entirely new, so that we may not even say that the life and
death and resurrection of Jesus Christ were a manifestation
in terms of space and time and human existence of what had
been eternally true. It was a new act of hitherto unaccom-
plished self-committal by God. See Phil. 2.5-11. In this
sense God *was* reconciling himself to us.

(ii) It was not enough that God should declare himself
loving towards us. Nor was it enough that we should see
the need of loving him and changing our attitude towards
him. Both of these things happened as a result of Christ's
work. But neither of them by themselves was enough; the
gulf between God and men was too great to be bridged merely
by a declaration of good intentions on both sides. Something had to be done, accomplished, to bring about reconciliation, something more than words and resolutions. Or,
to put it in another way, something had to be undone, re-
moved, overcome, put out of the way—the things which
were creating the barrier between God and man, things
in which were involved both God's majesty and man's
disobedience. These things Paul lists as Sin, Curse and
Death. The next verse tells us something of how this was
done.

**21. For he hath made him to be sin for us, who knew no
sin; that we might be made the righteousness of God in
him**

Compare Gal. 3.13, 'Christ hath redeemed us from the
curse of the law, being made a curse for us: for it is written,
Cursed is every one that hangeth on a tree.' God ordained

that Christ should become responsible for our sin, in so far
as he took on himself the full consequences of our sin—outlawry and death. The Law was a genuine ordinance of God
made necessary by human sin, and the Jew was convinced
that to be outside the Law was to cease to be well-pleasing
to God. Christ, says St. Paul, deliberately allowed himself
to be put outside the Law; it was his intention to put himself
in the place of sinners, to stand where sin was punished,
though he himself was personally sinless. MADE HIM TO
BE SIN must mean: 'treated as responsible for sin', and
therefore of course made to bear the consequence of sin.
Compare Rom. 8.3 (R.V.) 'God, sending his own Son in the
likeness of sinful flesh, and as an offering for sin, condemned
sin in the flesh.' So Christ endured the consequences of
outlawry and sin, making himself responsible for sin, and
enduring death, the end and destiny of sin. St. Paul, it
is clear, conceives our Lord as voluntarily consenting to
this process of reconciliation, when, for instance, he speaks
earlier in this chapter (v. 14) of 'the love of Christ', and in
many other places. To think otherwise would indeed make
nonsense of his theology. How far we can imagine Jesus
as having sympathy with and understanding of our sinful-
ness is, necessarily, an utter mystery, which St. Paul never
attempts to probe. We shall never fathom the depths of the
Messianic consciousness of Jesus.

Then in the Resurrection God demonstrated that sin and
death were powerless, broken, and on the wrong side (I Cor.
2.7, 8), and that Christ was on God's side, in fact that Christ
was the definition of what being on God's side, having God
with us, means (see Rom. 8.31-39). This being on God's
side, or God being with us or for us, is what lies behind
Paul's use of the words 'righteousness' and 'righteous',
when he applies them to men. We are MADE THE RIGHTEOUS-
NESS OF GOD IN HIM by being literally 'in' Christ, the
process beginning in Baptism and being renewed and
continued in Holy Communion. Compare I Cor. 1.30,
'But of him are ye in Christ Jesus, who of God is

made unto us wisdom, and righteousness, and sanctification, and redemption.'

Notice how, in explaining the work which an apostle has to do, Paul has to give a brief account of the whole reconciling work of God in Christ towards men. It is a sign that the apostolic ministry is an inseparable part of the gospel.

6.2. behold, now is the accepted time

In a parenthesis Paul betrays one of the fundamental assumptions of his gospel. He quotes Isa. 49.8, no doubt interpreting it as words addressed through the prophet by God to his Christ, and reminds the Corinthians that they are now living in the time when that prophecy is being fulfilled; cf. Rom. 1.1, 2 (' the gospel of God which he promised aforetime by his prophets in the holy scriptures ') and I Cor. 10.11 (' Now all these things happened unto them for examples, and they are written for our admonition, upon whom the ends of the world are come '). The Last Things—Judgment, Heaven, Hell—are not to Paul just a ' far-off divine event '; they are events which are happening to Christians *now*, in his own day. *Now* men and women are being saved (it is NOW THE DAY OF SALVATION); *now* men and women are being ruined. Now the destiny of each person is being decided according to their response to that final and irrevocable standard of judgment, Jesus Christ. It is true that the Arrival has not yet taken place, but the Arrival is the end of judgment and not the beginning of it; the Arrival is the announcement of the disappearance of the last chance, but *now*, this moment may be the Last Chance. Christians stand between the Cross and the End, between the inauguration of the Kingdom of God with the life, death and resurrection of the Messiah, and its consummation at his Arrival. All this period is the Last Time, the Ends of the Ages, the ACCEPTED TIME, tense with urgency, burning with hope, terrible with the possibilities of glory or ruin.

Våstly different though this may be from the complacent unconcern with which many Christians think about the Last Things during the season of Advent, this does represent St. Paul's view of them. And it is easy to see how consistent it is with the message of our Lord himself as reported in Mark 1.14, 15, or as taught in such parables as the Foolish Virgins (Matt. 25.1-13), and the Pearl of Great Price and the Treasure (Matt. 13.44-46).

7. It is probable that the Old Testament passage behind this is Isa. 59.17, as it certainly is behind Eph. 6.14-17.

on the right hand and the left
Moffatt translates: 'for attack or for defence'.

8-10. Another list of Interchange of qualities. The apostle shares the same paradox of humiliation and glory as does his Master.

NOTE ON THE BODY AND SOUL IN ST. PAUL'S THOUGHT

In our modern thought the words 'spirit' and 'soul' are virtually interchangeable, and mean something like, 'the essential personality', often thought of as immortal or as surviving death for a longer or shorter time. And when we speak about the phenomena of Spiritualism, it is significant that we talk in terms of the *spirit* surviving and of disembodied *spirits* or *souls*. But St. Paul does not seem to have thought of the human personality in exactly that way. He does not consistently divide the human personality at all, neither into 'soul and body', nor into 'spirit and flesh', nor into 'physical and mental', nor even into 'natural and supernatural'. For him, the human personality is one and indivisible. When he speaks of the 'spirit of a man' (as he does in I Cor. 2.10-16), this is not to draw a contrast between a man's body and a man's spirit; to St. Paul, 'body' usually meant the whole man, material and immaterial, considered as capable of redemption and glorification by God. And when he used the word ' flesh' to describe a person, he did not mean the carnal or physical aspect of a person, but the whole person considered as mortal, as sinful, and as separated from God. When he uses the word ' soul' of a person, it usually is either a simple equivalent to the word ' person' (as we would say, ' every *soul* on board the ship perished '; see Rom. 2.9; 13.1; II Cor. 1.23), or else means ' life' or ' breath of life' (e.g. Phil. 2.30; I Thess. 2.8); or else he uses it to mean ' the emotions ', rather as we use the word ' heart' in such a phrase as ' the desire of my heart' (e.g. Phil. 1.27; Col. 3.23; Eph. 6.6). It is true that in I Thess. 5.23 he says, 'I pray God your whole spirit and soul and body be preserved blameless unto the coming of our Lord Jesus Christ '. But this only means that he hopes that the Thessalonian Christians would be preserved alive until the Arrival, not that he expected a ' soul' to survive or to take part in the Resurrection. There is no clear example of Paul using ' soul' to mean ' essential personality '. To St. Paul the essential personality is the whole human being, not spirit apart from body, nor soul apart from body. And, if the essential personality is to survive death, then the whole human being must somehow survive death.

There can be little doubt that the phenomena investigated by Spiritualism would not have appeared to St. Paul as evidences of survival after death at all. He might well have said that they were *psychic*, i.e. connected with the ' soul' in his sense of the word, but that they had nothing to do with everlasting life given by the life-giving Spirit to Christians. And even modern Christians would be very wise to agree with him.

The phenomena of Spiritualism are *this-worldly* phenomena. Examples of dissociated or split personality spring to mind in this connection, and so do the messages from people who have apparently survived death, and even the appearances of ghosts, some of whose authenticity seems unimpeachable. If things connected with the 'soul', for instance intensely moving or disturbing experiences, or even patterns of behaviour which normally contribute towards forming a person's character, can in some at present unknown way become divorced from the essential person, either so that the person can leave them and return to them while still in this life (split personality), or so that they can in some way exist independently of the essential person after physical death for a greater or longer period (ghosts and spiritualistic phenomena), then we have got some sort of a clue to the meaning of these puzzling facts of split personalities and ghosts. In a word, at physical death the body gradually decays, and so also does the 'soul' (in St. Paul's sense), which may linger on in certain circumstances for some time and even be to some degree perceived or recognized by living people. If this were so, then spiritualistic phenomena would be decisively attached to *this* life, not to the next, and would have nothing to do with what the New Testament calls everlasting life, nor with spirits granted immortality by God. These phenomena would be merely a sort of psychological epilogue to the body, an emotional afterglow to the final sunset of physical existence, and nothing more. Certainly the contents of the messages purporting to come from personalities who have survived death and the behaviour of any well-authenticated ghosts would suggest by their triviality, limitedness and shallowness that they belong to some unexplored dimension of this life and not to the existence in Christ or in the nearer presence of God which the New Testament writers envisage as enjoyed by the human spirit after death. But if St. Paul's idea of the survival of the human personality is not that of the Spiritualists, how does he conceive of this survival? Well, it has already been made clear (see p. 43) that he half expected and half hoped that the Arrival of Jesus Christ would take place before physical death, in which case the human being, material and immaterial, would be transformed into a human being wholly devoted to and wholly fitted for the everlasting service of God, no longer hindered by a body destined to decay and a personality open to temptation and capable of sin; this new, Arrival, state of existence St. Paul calls 'the redemption of the body' (Rom. 8.23) or else 'the body of glory' (Phil. 3.21), or else 'a spiritual body' (I Cor. 15.44). But he always assumes that it will be an existence *in a body*, because he is convinced that we cannot live a full life wholly according to God's purpose unless we are in a body.

The Arrival, however, has not taken place as soon as St. Paul hoped that it might. What sort of survival are we to envisage between our individual physical deaths and the 'redemption of the body'? St. Paul is aware of this question, but he never has occasion in the letters that have come down to us to answer it directly. He speaks, as we have seen (see p. 43) of deceased Christians as those who are 'asleep in Christ' (I Cor. 15.18); he believes that if he dies himself before the Arrival he will be 'with Christ' (Phil. 1.23); and he says that we are not to sorrow for the Christian dead as people who have no hope, because at the Arrival God will bring them with Jesus (I Thess. 4.13, 14). But as for speaking of them in terms of body, soul or spirit—well he just has no occasion to do so, and we can learn virtually nothing from him in that respect. If the passage in II Cor. 5 discussed above means that during our life on earth our 'spiritual body' is gradually growing for us in Heaven, he may have thought that we receive it, or have some closer connection with it, when we die. This interpretation is attractive but not at all certain. Some scholars hold that Paul's view was that at physical death we leave our present bodies and receive instead the 'tabernacle' of *Christ's* Body; and they interpret the 'building from God, a house not made with hands, eternal, in the heavens' of II Cor. 5.1 as meaning Christ's Body.[1] But it seems too drastic a measure to interpret *all* St. Paul's references to the resurrection body as references to the Body of Christ and not to

[1] So J. A. T. Robinson in his brilliant little book, *The Body*.

any individual resurrection bodies.   Anyway II Cor. 5.1 very strongly suggests (with its clause ' if the earthly house of our tabernacle be dissolved ') that St. Paul does not think that Christians have this ' building from God ' as long as they are living in their present bodies; yet there are numerous passages where he either assumes or plainly states that they are *now* part of Christ's Body.[1]

On the details of this state of survival between death and resurrection, physical, metaphysical, psychical, or any other, we can, then, get no clear light from St. Paul.   But we do receive from him the overpowering impression that this survival is life ' with Christ ', which is, after all, all that we need to know.   This grand conviction, that the Saviour who has himself conquered death is perfectly capable of preserving us in life beyond the grave, however dim may necessarily be our conception of it, is the most important fact in forming the Christian's attitude to death, and in giving him the courage to look beyond it.

NOTE ON APOSTLESHIP

The question of what exactly constituted an apostle in the eyes of New Testament writers is a very uncertain, and indeed controversial one, because though the basic meaning of the word is clear enough, it is hard to find any consistent rule by which it seems to be applied in the New Testament.

Jesus was believed by the first Christians to be the ' apostle ', the plenipotentiary or representative, of God; the Epistle to the Hebrews actually gives our Lord this title (3.1), and it has been pointed out that the reason why St. John's Gospel never describes the Twelve as ' apostles ' is because the author prefers to reserve this title for Jesus

---

[1] I would single out I Cor. 6.15-17 as the most obvious of these.   That body which is here and now a member of Christ is capable of being joined to a harlot (and is therefore very much ' the earthly house of our tabernacle ').

himself. Still, the twelve men whom Jesus chose as his
disciples in a special way and whom he commissioned
clearly were intended to be apostles of Jesus as Jesus was
the apostle of God. They were the church, in nucleus.
They were the foundation, the historical beginning, unique
in their position in history, of the new people of God, the
twelve new patriarchs of the new Israel (Matt. 19.28; Rev.
21.14).

The difficulties arise when we try to determine what
exactly this word meant after the Ascension and Pentecost,
in the first century of the Church's existence. Not only do
we know nothing at all about the fate of more than half the
Twelve (Peter, James, John, and Judas are the only names
mentioned in Acts, and of these James and John appear only
fleetingly); but other people whom we do not know to have
been commissioned by Jesus himself are treated as if they
were so commissioned. It is easy enough to agree that
Paul's case is exceptional; indeed he declared it to be so
himself. He was commissioned ' an apostle of Jesus Christ '
in the fullest sense by a special appearance of Jesus Christ
vouchsafed to him (Gal. 1.11-16; I Cor. 9.1; 15.7-9). Nobody
could accuse him of failing to insist that his apostolic
authority was as genuine as any man's. His description of
himself in almost all his letters, and particularly his defence
of his apostleship in I and II Corinthians, make this quite
clear. But what about his description of James the Lord's
brother (not the apostle James, brother of John, son of
Zebedee, who was martyred early on, about the year 44 by
Herod Agrippa; Acts 12.2) as an apostle, and as an apostle
who had seen the Lord (Gal. 1.19; I Cor. 15.7)? How is it
that Paul can describe Apollos as an apostle, and that
not, apparently, merely as representative of some particular
group for some temporary purpose, but as one who like
himself had spoken the word of reconciliation to the Corinthians, had had part in their conversion?[1] It is very hard
to imagine that Apollos had ' seen the Lord ' as Peter or

---

[1] I can draw no other conclusions from I Cor. 4.6, 9 and ff.

even as Paul himself had. How is it that Barnabas is described as an apostle with Paul in Acts 14.4, 14?

No final, cut-and-dried answer can be given to this question. Modern scholarship has certainly not yet made up its mind on the point. Perhaps we may make a provisional distinction between three types of 'apostle' in the New Testament:

1. Anybody who was the commissioned representative of any person or group of persons for some specified purpose and limited period of time (Rom. 16.7; II Cor. 8.23; Phil. 2.25).

2. The 'apostles of Jesus Christ', men who had been in some way or at some point commissioned by Jesus Christ (perhaps through the Spirit) to minister the word of reconciliation, to convert men and women to his gospel, to bring them into his Church. Some, but not all, of these would be men who had 'seen the Lord' after the Resurrection.[1] Paul obviously distinguishes between 'a brother' and 'an apostle of Jesus Christ', not only in I Cor. 15.6-9, but also in I Cor. 1.1; II Cor. 1.1; and in Col. 1.1. In this category would be included Apollos and Barnabas, and indeed Paul himself. With this view would fit in Paul's occasional assumption (e.g. I Cor. 9.2, 3; II Cor. 12.12) that an apostle has to be proved an apostle by his activity on behalf of his Lord.

3. The Twelve, i.e. the original twelve apostles, less Judas and with the addition of Matthias. Paul clearly makes a

[1] This of course involves assuming that St. Paul does not regard the experience of seeing Jesus after the Resurrection as an invariable qualification for being an 'apostle of Jesus Christ'. I Cor. 9.1 and 15.6-9, if closely examined, can be seen not necessarily to involve this assumption. In 9.1 'Am I not free, am I not an apostle? Have I not seen Jesus our Lord? Are not you my work in the Lord?' do not all necessarily mean that his having seen the Lord made him an apostle, any more than his being free made him an apostle. What made him so was the commission he received when he saw the Lord. In 15.7-9 Paul's statement that Jesus appeared (i) to Peter, (ii) to the Twelve, (iii) to five hundred brethren, (iv) to James, (v) to all the apostles and (vi) to Paul would *a priori* suggest that 'the apostles' were not the Twelve and that they were apostles before the Lord appeared to them, and that others besides apostles had 'seen the Lord'.

distinction and puts the Twelve in a category by themselves in Gal. 2.6-9; I Cor. 15.6-9 (and possibly, though not certainly, II Cor. 11.5 and 12.11). Perhaps, in view of Gal. 2.6-9, we should add James the Lord's brother to this number. He may have been accounted as equivalent to an apostle, as he was of the family of Jesus and, according to Acts and the ecclesiastical historian Eusebius, played a very important part in the Church in Jerusalem of the first generation. It is even possible that Paul accounts him to be the twelfth apostle, and not Matthias.

The further question of whether these apostles, of any category, appointed successors, and if so how, is an even more complicated one, and cannot be more than glanced at here. It must be remembered that apostleship is a function, not an office; that is, it is a task to be done, not a post to be filled, just as in the British Government the position of Prime Minister is not a position but a function (it has no salary attached to it). We must not therefore think of it as a post to which somebody must be appointed when the present holder of it dies or retires. In the case of the 'apostle' of the first category noted above, it is obvious that there could be no question of a successor. And there could evidently be no exact successor to one of the Twelve, the distinguishing mark of whom was that each member had been a companion of the Lord in the days of his earthly Ministry.

But successors to the sort of apostleship that St. Paul wrote of as his in II Corinthians and as his and Apollos' in I Corinthians, there obviously could be, indeed there must be. This ministry of the word of reconciliation, this standing between God and men as ambassadors, must be continued if the Church was to be continued. Is there any evidence in the New Testament that provision was made for its continuance? There is a certain amount of evidence, but its interpretation is very uncertain. There is no evidence at all that anybody called 'apostle' appoints somebody else to succeed him officially as an apostle, but the fact that this was a function and not an office might well account for that.

There is fairly clear evidence that 'apostles' appointed 'elders' (or 'presbyters') in local churches (Acts 14.23; 15.4, 6, 23; 20.17), and that these elders had (or at the very least were by a later age supposed to have had) pastoral oversight and responsibility very similar to that which Paul ascribes to an apostle (Paul's speech to the elders of Ephesus at Miletus in Acts 20.17-36 makes this very likely). There are also mentioned officials called *episkopoi* (literally 'overseers'; 'bishops' is a rather anachronistic description of them), and it is almost impossible to avoid the conclusion that these officials were identical with elders. In Acts 20.17 St. Paul is said to have summoned the elders of Ephesus to meet him, and in the speech which he delivers to them he says (v. 28), 'Take heed therefore unto yourselves, and to all the flock, over the which the Holy Ghost hath made you overseers' (*episkopoi*). And a careful reading of Titus 1.5-7 should convince the readers that the author (who was probably not St. Paul, but somebody living at a considerably later date than he) intended exactly the same people by the 'elders' in verse 5 and the 'bishop' in verse 7. Further, St. Paul does not once mention 'elders' in an official sense in his letters, but he does once refer to bishops as officials of a local church (Phil. 1.1). The probability therefore is strong that 'apostles of Jesus Christ' did appoint local elders or overseers to exercise apostleship like theirs locally. Whether there ever were single elder-overseers appointed to succeed a single apostle, or whether they were at first always appointed in groups, is a subject beyond the scope of this Note.

The apparent inconsistencies in the use of the word 'apostle' in the New Testament, however, become much less important if we adopt the view advanced by A. T. Hanson (in his book *The Pioneer Ministry*) that the main function of apostleship is to communicate apostolicity to the rest of the Church. The apostle carries out his function of communicating light in order that those who have received the light may share in the apostolic task of spreading that light. The purpose of the ministry is to equip all Christians for ministry . . . We are both served by the apostolic ministry and must ourselves join in that service. The ministry then is not something given to the Church from outside to create and hold it together; it is rather something given in the Church by Christ to be the Church, to be and do that which the Church, following it, must be and do (*The Pioneer Ministry*, p. 105). This would explain how there are different sorts of apostles, as apostleship spreads further in the infant Church, and yet how there must always be an apostolic ministry within the Church.

II

A FRAGMENT OF ANOTHER LETTER
6.14–7.1

The reasons for setting these verses aside as a fragment of another letter which has become mixed up with the longer one lie in the inconsequence and apparent pointlessness of introducing the theme of these verses at this point, and the remarkably apt correspondence of 6.13 with 7.2. This is how the verses run in the Revised Standard Version: ' You are not restricted by us, but you are restricted in your own affections. In return—I speak as to children—widen your hearts also. Open your hearts to us; we have wronged no one, we have corrupted no one. . . .' But in between ' widen your hearts also ' and ' Open your hearts to us ' come these six apparently quite irrelevant verses urging the Corinthians not to contract marriages with pagans, because this will bring them into contact with the unclean influences of pagan ethics and religion. Many commentators have professed to see a connection of thought here, and some even a natural and close connection, but their ingenuity is greater than their power of conviction. The best alternative theory is that St. Paul, dictating the letter, suddenly realized that he must deal with the subject of Marriage with Unbelievers, and threw in these few words, immediately afterwards resuming the main thread of his discourse. But this is rather more difficult to envisage than the theory that these verses are a fragment from another letter. The suggestion that this fragment came from the letter mentioned in I Cor. 5.9 is an interesting one. The question of how such a fragment could

have got written into the main letter is touched on in the
Introduction (pp. 17-21).

14. Be not unequally yoked

In the Revised Standard Version is translated: ' Do not
be mismated ', and Moffatt translates it: ' Keep out of all
incongruous ties.'

6.15-7.1. Observe the immense conviction evident in all St.
Paul's letters and throughout the New Testament, that
Christians are the new Israel of God, chosen, called, elect
people, in whom God himself dwells.   This—the living
presence of the Holy Spirit in the Church—is the Real
Presence of the New Testament, and the reason why there
is no doctrine of the ' Real Presence ' in the Bible.   St. Paul
ranges the whole Old Testament to support his plea, calling
indiscriminately on Leviticus and Ezekiel (v. 16), Isaiah,
Jeremiah, Ezekiel again and Zephaniah (v. 17), II Samuel,
Jeremiah again, Isaiah again and Hosea (v. 18).   In his view
the whole Old Testament spoke directly to the Christian
about his status in Christ.   It was this conviction of separate-
ness, calling, and purpose in God which gave the Christian
Church its immense power to survive and to spread during
the first centuries of its existence.

III

THE MAIN LETTER CONTINUED

ST. PAUL RESUMES THE ACCOUNT OF HIS MOVEMENTS AND MOTIVES
6.11-13 and 7.2-16

6.12, 13. The A.V. translation here is, to our minds, grotesquely archaic and even three hundred years ago must have sounded strangely. The R.V. is little better. The Revised Standard Version runs: ' You are not restricted in us, but you are restricted in your own affections. In return —I speak as to children—widen your hearts also.' Moffatt translates v. 13: ' A fair exchange, now! as the children say,' which is very vivid.

7.6. God that comforteth those that are cast down

Even in a little phrase like this St. Paul speaks from a rich Old Testament background; Isa. 49.13 he quotes; and such passages as Ps. 138.6; 113.6, and Zeph. 3.12 may be in his mind.

8, 9. The punctuation, and consequently the translation, adopted by the A.V., R.V., and the Revised Standard Version here are difficult and unsatisfactory. The verse should probably run something like this: ' Because even if I did upset you by my letter, I am not sorry for it; even if at one time I was sorry for it, I perceive that that letter, even if it did upset you temporarily—well I am glad it did now, not because you were upset, but because your being upset brought you to the point of being sorry.'

E

10. A brilliant statement of the infinitely great difference between remorse (which is not specifically Christian) and repentance (which is wholly Christian).

11. Revenge is an impossible translation in the context. R.V. ' avenging ' is little better; ' punishment ' (Revised Standard Version) or ' exacting of satisfaction ' is more adequate.

12. Note the slight but significant change in the R.V. which translates ' that *your* earnest care for *us* might be made manifest unto you ', instead of the A.V.'s OUR CARE FOR YOU. Paul wanted the Corinthians to realize how much they really cared for him.   The R.V. translation is based on a better reading.

13. Once again the punctuation of the A.V. is unsatisfactory. The first four words of this verse really belong to the preceding verse, and the passage should run: ' therefore [i.e. because of what v. 12 had described] have we been encouraged. And in addition to our encouragement we rejoiced immensely more at Titus' joy. . . .'

THE CONTRIBUTION TO THE
JERUSALEM CHURCH
8 and 9

Encouraged by the generosity of the Macedonian churches, St. Paul makes bold to ask the Corinthian church to contribute to the fund he is raising for the poor Christians of Jerusalem, as a proof of the sincerity of their affection. Several points in these chapters need to be noted first: (i) With what extreme circumspection and almost gushing geniality Paul makes this request!   Obviously he knows that he is liable to be accused of being a ' pedlar of God's word ' (2.17, Revised Standard Version).   He carefully explains that he is not giving commands in this matter (I SPEAK NOT

BY COMMANDMENT, 8.8; AND HEREIN I GIVE MY ADVICE, 8.10; cf. I Cor. 7.6). When he speaks with full apostolic authority, as in Galatians and later in II Corinthians, he can command (contrast II Cor. 13.2, 10), but in fact he seldom does so. He hardly ever lays down a rule, but prefers to elucidate principles, and lay the responsibility of choice on his individual converts. Compare the way in which he deals with the problem of eating meat offered to idols in I Cor. 8 and with the question of fasting and sabbath-observance in Rom. 14.

(ii) Observe the varied and yet consistent uses of the word GRACE in chapter 8. In vv. 6, 7, and 19 it means a gift; in v. 4 it means the privilege of giving; in v. 9 it means the undeserved love of Christ manifested in his Incarnation; in v. 16 it means thanks. Though the word is translated GIFT in v. 4 and THANKS in v. 16, it is the same word in every context in Greek—*charis*. *Charis* is the unearned, unexpected, free love of God declared in Christ's self-emptying; in the lives of Christians it expresses itself in a giving which is at once a privilege (as it is a sharing in Christ's *charis*) and an act of thanksgiving.

(iii) Observe one more example of the Interchange in Christ which we have already noted (pp. 30-3); chapter 8 speaks in several places of the Interchange of Poverty and Wealth which Christians take on themselves (vv. 2, 9, 13, 14). The Corinthians give now, not as richer members condescending to give to their poorer brethren, but as brothers who know that, in Christ, their present supplying of the needs of the Christians of Jerusalem will be answered by the people of Jerusalem in some way and at some time supplying their need.

8.1. We do you to wit of

R.V. translates as 'make known to you'.

2. Liberality

This word occurs more in II Cor. than in any other book

of the New Testament (its use is in fact confined to St.
Paul), and all its occurrences in II Cor. except one (11.3, a
significant exception, as we shall see) occur in these two
chapters. In these it always means 'willingness' or 'simple
kindness' and refers to people's readiness to give. In this
chapter, Paul dwells mainly on the touching readiness of the
already very poor Macedonian churches (presumably of
Philippi, Thessalonica and Beroea) to contribute to his fund;
in chapter 9 he stresses the readiness to give which he knows
(or professes to know) to exist among the Corinthians.

6. A year ago the Corinthians had suggested or initiated this
Collection, and Titus had been put in charge of it. In v. 10
St. Paul delicately suggests that they should get on with it.

9. In the middle of a passage devoted to the very mundane
business of trying to extract money from the Corinthians,
Paul slips in quite casually a moving reference to the self-
humiliation of our Lord in the Incarnation. This was not because he felt that he must diversify a very material affair with
some spiritual interludes, but because for St. Paul the material,
the mundane and the everyday is (or should be) an expression
of the spiritual. Life was not for him divided into a spiritual
realm on the one hand where the Christian can meet God in
religious experience and escape from material and outward
things, and on the other a hard, uninteresting, unsanctified
material realm where the Christian has to get on as well as
he can. For St. Paul the outward, the physical, the material,
the ordinary necessities of human existence, were the natural
expression of God's power and character. Observe too that
St. Paul knows nothing of a distinction between ordinary
Christianity and more advanced and difficult 'dogma'. To
him the most advanced, the most offensive, the most difficult
dogma of all—the Incarnation and Atonement of our Lord
Jesus Christ—is the very centre and heart of Christianity.
The Incarnation (HE BECAME POOR) and the Atonement (THAT
YE THROUGH HIS POVERTY MIGHT BE RICH) underlies this

exhortation to Christian giving, which is indeed a marvel of compressed dogma. Incidentally the verse serves to make clear St. Paul's conviction that Jesus Christ was not a man specially gifted or favoured by God, but a Being who had existed before he took human form among us; cf. Phil. 2.5-11.

15. He adorns his argument by a quotation from Ex. 16.18, a description of the miraculously self-regulating (almost thermostatic) capacity of the manna gathered by the people of Israel in the wilderness to meet the need of everybody, without overwhelming the man who needed little nor failing the man who needed much. This phenomenon, St. Paul implies, was a foretaste or prophecy of the self-adjusting love of Christ in His members which supplies the need of each without deficiency or embarrassment.

17-24. Paul commends each of the messengers who have recently visited the Corinthian community.

17. he accepted the exhortation
That is, he agreed with my suggestion that he should go to you, carrying this letter.

18. the brother, whose praise is in the gospel
We do not of course know who is meant by this phrase. The Book of Common Prayer, in its Collect for St. Luke's Day, identifies him with St. Luke, following some early guesses. If Luke wrote the Third Gospel and the Book of Acts (which is very likely) and *if* the same Luke was using his own travel-diary, not some other man's, when he wrote the passages in Acts which can be recognized as an eye-witness' account of the events described (which is quite another matter and not nearly as simple as the other), there is considerable probability in this guess. But these *ifs* remove us far from certainty on the point. St. Paul does not of course mean that this 'brother's' praise is in the gospel

which he has written, because no gospel (not even the earliest, St. Mark's) could have been written by this time. He means that this man's praise lies in the way in which he has forwarded the propagation of the gospel.

19-21. This 'brother' was not merely sent by St. Paul. He was the official representative ('messenger' or 'apostle', he calls him, along with the other 'brother') of all the churches who were organizing this Collection. And he, along with another 'brother', alluded to in v. 22, was sent in order to guarantee to the churches from whom the Collection was to be taken that St. Paul was acting in an honourable and disinterested way. This is what Paul means by his quotation of Prov. 3.4 in v. 21.

22. The name of this other BROTHER is likewise unknown. Of the three who were to bring this letter to Corinth, Titus was obviously most closely attached to Paul, the other two being representatives of the churches rather than of the apostle.

9.3. Yet have I sent the brethren
Even though these men are MESSENGERS OF THE CHURCHES (8.23) Paul now describes them as sent by him, because they go with his consent, to vindicate his character and to carry his letter.

11-15. Paul lifts the affair of the Collection out of the atmosphere of calculation and ulterior motive by describing it as a sacrificial giving involved in Christ's sacrifice whereby Christians are exchanging love and unselfishness and gratitude among themselves, and thanksgiving is given continually as a consequence to God. He has sounded very much the same note in chapter 1.11.

12. the administration of this service
Literally the deaconing of this liturgy. Paul is deliberately

using the language of ministration at a religious sacrifice (pagan as well as Jewish) in connection with this charitable work of the Collection, as he does elsewhere of other work done in the name of Christ (see Rom. 12.1; 15.16). What is done in Christ's name is a re-application, a re-declaration, a re-manifestation of Christ's sacrifice. This would of course apply to Christian worship as well as to Christian activity in other fields. It is impossible to imagine that the early Church envisaged itself as manifesting Christ's sacrifice in alms-giving and social service, but carefully dropped this idea when they came together to worship. This is not to say that Paul regarded himself as what we would now call ' a sacrific-ing priest '. The fact that in this passage the people who are involved in the sacrificial activity are the Corinthian Chris-tians should dispose of that idea. Christ had offered—was offering—his one, effective, final sacrifice. All Christians (' brothers ' as well as apostles) were involved in the appli-cation and manifestation of that sacrifice, for all were *in* Christ. It is continually necessary to remember that, for St. Paul, Christians were not merely followers of Christ, not merely imitators of his example or practisers of his teach-ing, but were members of his body, people living a new life in a new creation constituted by his Person.

15. On this almost lyrical note Paul's treatment of the Col-lection ends. It is morally impossible that from such appar-ent contentment and joy he should without warning switch to the anxious chiding of the next three chapters.

CONCLUSION
13.11-14

The reasons for concluding that these verses were originally part of the longest, and probably the latest, of the three letters which we have assumed to compose II Corinthians have been briefly stated in the Introduction (see pp. 17-20).

We would only note here that the tone of vv. 11-14 is mild, gentle and loving, fitting admirably in with a letter which has reached its penultimate paragraph at 9.15, but not nearly so appropriate to the stern tone and crisp menace of 13.1-10. Paul is quite capable of ending a letter without terms of endearment if he wants to; see Gal. 6.11-18.

14. The fact that this verse is not designedly 'Trinitarian' is a strong argument for 'Trinitarian' doctrine. In other words, St. Paul is not here trying to end his letter with a text which will show his belief in the Christian doctrine of the Holy Trinity, Three Persons and one God, because this doctrine was not formulated in this form for centuries after his death. But it does show that words which, logically developed, form the basis of such a doctrine do most naturally come into his mind when he wants to sum up his gospel.

IV

PART OF ANOTHER LETTER
(probably the ' Severe Letter ')
10.1–13.10

As we study these chapters we must bear in mind that they almost certainly represent another letter from the preceding chapters, and probably the one referred to in 2.3, 4, the ' Severe Letter ', written OUT OF MUCH AFFLICTION AND ANGUISH OF HEART, WITH MANY TEARS. We are now reading words written in a quite different situation, psychologically as well as geographically. He is writing from Ephesus to a Christian community whom he has just visited, writing to reproach them for their bad treatment of him during his visit, and to reassert and vindicate his apostolic authority over them, which some of them have seriously questioned. He knows that there is a party in Corinth opposed to him.

A MILD OPENING OF THE OFFENSIVE
10

1. base
Is a bad translation; R.V. ' lowly ' is better.

2. I beseech you, that I may not be bold
Is undoubtedly a literal translation of the Greek, but does it make sense? The R.V. which virtually reproduces it, seems to think so, but, unless we translate ' I beseech you to prevent me being bold ' (which is more than the words justify), the sentiment is an impossible one. The Revised

Standard Version and Moffatt acknowledge this by trans-
lating: 'that I may not *have to* show boldness' (so the
Revised Standard Version; 'to speak out' is Moffatt's
rendering); this makes sense, but is a paraphrase, not a
translation. Possibly the words should be translated, 'I beg
of you that I may not desire when I am present to be
aggressive.'

Some which think of us as if we walked according to the flesh

This is the first mention of St. Paul's opponents. He
accuses them, as later chapters reveal, of estimating him in a
purely worldly way, according to the magnetism of his
personality, or his influential connections, or his startling
and unusual spiritual experiences. He here refuses to be
judged by these standards; he has authority from God to
dissipate such illusory ways of looking at things. For the
meaning of ACCORDING TO THE FLESH see also the note on
5.16 (pp. 48-9) and the note at the beginning of the Section
11.16–12.10 (pp. 81-2).

3. We do not war after the flesh

No, but Paul admits that he does 'war'; the fight, so to
speak, is on, and the military metaphor of the next two
verses is not inappropriate.

6. When the Corinthians acknowledge their obligation to
listen to St. Paul, then he will have an opportunity of punish-
ing their present disobedience.

7. If any man trust himself that he is Christ's

This might well be a reference to the party who in I Cor.
1.12 are described as claiming 'I am of Christ'.

8-12. 'I intend to pay you a visit,' St. Paul here implies, 'and
you must not imagine that when I come I will be unable to
assert myself, as you appear to think I was at my last visit.

You must not imagine that though I can write stern letters
I will always give way in a personal interview. I intend to
assert my authority.' This matter of *authority* was indeed
the whole point of this letter, and he reverts to this point
again in the very last verse of it which has survived (13.10).

8. Edification means ' building up ', a constructive and not
merely negative activity. Paul is convinced that, whatever
his personal shortcomings, he has been given this authority
by God and in this situation he is bound to assert it.

12. ' The Pharisees took for granted exactly the point at
issue. They assumed that the divine standard of righteousness was the Mosaic law, as they had come to interpret it.
Their spiritual pride was due to the fact that they judged
themselves simply by this standard, no Pharisee comparing
himself with anybody except other Pharisees. . . . St. Paul
could in fact claim for himself all that they claimed (cf.
11.22, 23; Phil. 3.5, 6); but the law itself led him to die to
the law (Gal. 2.19). Facing, as the Pharisees did not, the
real divine standard, he found that it led him, not to self-
congratulation, but to self-despair; and so was ready for the
gospel of redemption by the Cross ' (Goudge).[1]

13-16. These verses are some of the most difficult in the
whole work to translate. THINGS WITHOUT OUR MEASURE is
a very odd phrase; if ' without ' means ' lacking ', then the
phrase is meaningless; if we translate ' beyond ', which is the
way the R.V., Revised Standard Version, and Moffatt translate it, then we get good sense, but the Greek hardly justifies
such a rendering. It is probably best to take the whole
phrase as meaning ' excessively ' or ' inordinately '. It is
clear that Paul is protesting that in claiming the Corinthians'
obedience he is not going beyond what he has a right to
claim, nor impinging upon an area of work proper to some
other apostle, and that he regards himself as free even to

[1] *The Second Epistle to the Corinthians*, p. 97.

make them a base for further evangelization if he receives the necessary encouragement. We might paraphrase these verses thus:

> ' We will not make inordinate claims, but according to the order of that mandate which was the order that God ordered for us we claim that we have reached as far as you. For we are not straining ourselves as if we did not really reach you, for we have already attained as far as you in the gospel of Christ. We are not making inordinate claims upon another man's sphere of labour, but we cherish a hope that as your faith increases we shall be promoted by you, keeping to our mandate, for something further—to preach the gospel in the regions beyond you without intruding upon another man's mandate and making claims upon work near at hand.'

For this refusal to evangelize where other apostles had already evangelized, and for St. Paul's desire to go further, see Rom. 15.20, 21, 23, 24.

A SARCASTIC ATTACK ON HIS MAIN OPPONENT
11.1-15

11.1. Folly

Does not mean ' silliness ' so much as affectation or acting a part from unworthy motives. In this chapter Paul several times argues as if he was assuming that he had the same selfish motives and worldly outlook as his opponents, but he always warns his hearers by using this word ' foolishness ' or some cognate of it (cf. 11.16, 17, 19, 21, 23; 12.6, 11).

and indeed bear with me

Must be a reinforcement of the first words of this verse; it cannot be a statement that in fact the Corinthians are sympathetic towards his point of view.

2. Here St. Paul uses the figure of a bridegroom and bride to describe the relation of Christ to the Church, for the ONE HUSBAND is Christ. He is not only the Bridegroom of the Church (Eph. 5.25-33), but also of each particular local church (as is evident from this passage) and also of each individual Christian (I Cor. 6.13-17). For this conception St. Paul had a rich Old Testament background in the often-repeated picture of God as the Bridegroom of Israel; see Hosea 2.19, 20; Isa. 54.3, 6; Jer. 3.1. It is possible that it was some words of our Lord which gave St. Paul the cue for using this traditional figure; see Mark 2.18-20; Matt. 25.1-18. The figure is used again by the author of Revelation (19.6-9). It is a most appropriate image, as the uses of it by St. Paul show, for the closeness of intimacy and inviolability of the union of the Christian with his Saviour.

3. The 'new Eve' in St. Paul's thought is the Church, *not* the Blessed Virgin Mary. The tradition of describing St. Mary as the New Eve, on the grounds that through her salvation entered the world, as sin through Eve, is first found only in Justin, who was martyred about 165 A.D. Paul regards Adam as the origin of sin, in contrast to the Second Adam, Jesus Christ, the origin of salvation (see Rom. 5.12-21; I Cor. 15.45-49). And his comparing of the Church to Eve in this context is far from flattering; she may be the New Eve, he implies, but she is behaving alarmingly like the old Eve.

Simplicity

This is the same word in Greek (*haplotes*) as occurred in 8.2 and 9.11, 13, meaning 'liberality', 'kindness in giving' (see note on 8.2, pp. 67-8). Here it means 'innocence' or 'purity', and provides one more small piece of evidence that these chapters come from a different letter. If Paul had praised the *haplotes* of the Corinthians in chapter 9, he is not likely to cast suspicion on their *haplotes* in the same letter without explanation.

4. This verse raises a series of difficulties:

(i) Who is HE THAT COMETH? If we rely on parallels in other parts of the New Testament (e.g. Luke 7.19; Rev. 1.4; 4.8), we might expect it to refer to some mysterious divine figure, perhaps God himself. But it would be unwise to follow these parallels too readily in this context. It might mean some single opponent of Paul at Corinth who had come in from outside. But it is more likely to mean *anyone* who comes in from outside claiming to bring an authoritative message to the Corinthians. The Revised Standard Version translates: ' But if someone comes and preaches . . .' and Moffatt renders the phrase ' some interloper '.

(ii) The meaning of the words translated in the A.V. YE MIGHT WELL BEAR WITH HIM is ambiguous, but the A.V. translation is almost certainly wrong. The Greek for this phrase literally means according to the best reading: ' you put up with very well ' (*not* ' you might put up with '). Now, St. Paul *may* have been speaking in a quite straightforward manner and may have actually intended to applaud the Corinthians for putting up with some outsider preaching another gospel, but the general context makes this very improbable. The probability is that Paul is here writing in a slightly ironical way, and intends a contrast between the remarkably tolerant way in which his converts will endure the teaching of some outsider who brings a message which is alien from the true gospel, and their critical and truculent attitude towards him. The Revised Standard Version translates the phrase: ' you submit to it readily enough.'

(iii) Who are the people against whom Paul is writing? We presume, for reasons just stated, that it is not just one opponent, but a party, opposed to him. Who *exactly* these were we can never know, because, like so many points in this work, our only source of knowledge is, as it were, a dialogue between Paul and the Corinthians overheard by us, in which he assumes their knowledge of all sorts of events which are unknown to us. But the language which Paul here uses of his opponents is so much like that which he used of the opponents against whom he was writing in the Epistle to the Galatians that it is reasonable to conclude that they were the same sort of person (see Gal. 1.6-9). If so, they were Judaizing Christians, trying to convert the Corinthians to a type of Christianity in which observance of the whole of the Jewish Law would be compulsory, and claiming an authority greater than Paul's as conferred direct by the greatest figures in the Christian Church, Peter and James in Jerusalem (the whole of Gal. 1 and 2 illustrates this situation). We shall be able to infer something more about these people as we read on through the Letter.

(iv) Notice St. Paul's three-word summary of Christianity —Jesus, Spirit, Gospel. It is a little disconcerting for us to realize that he does not summarize Christianity as 'Father, Son, Spirit', nor as 'Jesus, Mary, Church', nor as 'Love, Joy, Peace', nor as 'Liberty, Equality, Fraternity', nor in any way particularly palatable to modern thought. Jesus— the New Creation; Spirit—the New Life in which to live in this Creation; Gospel—the instrument for spreading this life in this Creation; this is what St. Paul thinks Christianity consists of.

5. The very chiefest apostles

Paul cannot in this phrase be referring directly to Peter and James and the original Eleven, because he had quite recently, writing to these same Corinthians, described them as official witnesses of the Resurrection (I Cor. 15.5-7), and in Galatians, though it is obvious that he does not mind opposing Peter and James where he thinks it necessary, he is very far from referring to them as 'false apostles, deceitful workers, transforming themselves into the apostles of Christ', which is his description a few verses later on of those whom he here calls the VERY CHIEFEST APOSTLES (II

Cor. 11.13). These people must be his immediate opponents in Corinth, men who have come to Corinth claiming to be authorized representatives of the Twelve, with authority overriding Paul's. Such men might well have claimed that their strictly Jewish form of Christianity represented the true tradition of the original apostles (all of them Palestinian Jews) in contrast to Paul's Gentile corruptions of the faith.

6. Rude in speech

'Rude' is a most unfortunate word for both the A.V. and the R.V. to use, because to the average person to-day it means either 'offensive' or 'obscene'. 'Unskilled' or 'unqualified' is a better translation. It probably implies that St. Paul had not been educated in oratory according to the usual Greek method. A modern parallel might be: 'without a degree in Arts'.

I robbed other churches

A characteristically Pauline exaggeration. He apparently means that he took more from other Christian communities than was strictly necessary for his support.

9. I was chargeable to no man

The Greek verb literally means, to be or grow numb. The R.V. translation is better: I was not a burden to any man. It is worth noting how very ill this emphasis accords with the supposition that this chapter is part of the same letter as chapters 8 and 9, where he is plainly, though tactfully, doing something which exposes him to the very charge that he here disavows—the charge of trying to extract money from the Corinthians.

12. Another verse rendered obscure by our ignorance of the state of affairs to which it is alluding. It is not likely that St. Paul's opponents charged him with not really caring for his converts because he did not ask them to pay for him (which would imply a rather queer proof of affection). They

probably accused him of acknowledging that he was no true
apostle because he was afraid to demand the apostle's right
of maintenance by his spiritual children (see I Cor. 9.1-12).
In this verse he is saying that his opponents want him to drop
the practice of abstaining from asking support from his converts, so that they (who do demand such support) may be
on the same footing as he, and so to confirm their claim to
apostleship.   Both the A.V. and R.V. translations here are,
therefore, unsatisfactory.   The Revised Standard Version
runs: ' And what I do I will continue to do, in order to under-
mine the claim of those who would like to claim that in their
boasted mission they work on the same terms as we do.'

A COMPARISON OF HIS OWN CLAIMS AND ACHIEVEMENTS WITH THOSE OF HIS OPPONENTS
11.16–12.10

Paul now justifies his remark in 11.1 (see note on this on
p. 76) by making for a time the outlook of his opponents
his own, and showing that even from the point of view of
worldly and selfish ambition he has a greater claim on
allegiance of the Christians; he has as good credentials of
birth and education as they, and vastly more on the score of
what he has done and suffered for the faith.   Assuming for a
moment that he is the 'fool' (11.1, 16, 17, 19, 21, 23; 12.11)
which his opponents no doubt accused him of being, and
assuming that it was a matter of debate whether the Corinthians should 'put up with' him (11.1, 4, 19, 20), as his
opponents had no doubt insisted, he shows that even on this
hypothesis his claim annihilates theirs.   ' I am now deliberately making selfish, worldly, competitive claims,' St. Paul
in effect says, ' I am descending to the level of my opponents
and showing that even on the level of sheer worldly merit or
achievement I am superior to them.'   But he cannot keep it
up, and while he is describing what he has suffered in Christ's
name (11.23-33), we feel that he has transcended this tem-

F

porary phase of worldliness (see 11.30) and is anticipating the magnificent claim of 12.10 and 13.3, 4 that WHEN I AM WEAK, THEN AM I STRONG.

It is evident that his opponents accused Paul of being a fool, questioned his apostolic authority and urged the Corinthians not to put up with him. And 12.1-10 makes it clear that they claimed their visions and impressive spiritual experience as a sign of their genuineness and superiority.

18. After the flesh, see note on 5.16 (pp. 48-9).

It is possible that the word HENCEFORTH in 5.16 implies that in an earlier letter (this ' Severe Letter ') he had deliberately spoken and thought AFTER THE FLESH, and that he is now renouncing this behaviour.

20. A description of what the Corinthians had been quite uncomplainingly putting up with from his opponents. BRING YOU INTO BONDAGE probably refers to the interlopers' teaching that the Corinthians must keep all the Jewish Law (cf. Gal. 5.1).

devour

Means : ' use up all your available resources ', presumably by demanding the right to live free.

smite you on the face

May be meant literally (cf. Acts 23.1-2), but the Greek phrase can be taken metaphorically to mean ' fly in your face '.

21. I speak as concerning reproach, as though we had been weak

Most recent commentaries take this as a very ironical remark, assuming that St. Paul is sarcastically apologizing for not being able to descend to the level of his opponents (' I am quite ashamed to say I was not equal to that sort of thing '—Moffatt). But this very bitter sarcasm seems alto-

gether too subtle, especially as Paul all through this passage
explains in asides that he is indulging in the artificial role of
boaster, and this looks remarkably like such an aside.   The
sentence could be better translated, ' I speak this to shame
you, as if we had sunk as low as they '.   For this sense of
' weak ', meaning ' sinful ' compare Rom. 5.6, and v. 29 of
this chapter.

23. I am more
' I am more so ', not ' I am more than a minister '.

23-33. When St. Paul does come to make his claims ' according to the flesh ', how unanswerable, how magnificent they
are!   In spite of, indeed because of, an unparalleled experience of adventures with gangsters and fanatics, disasters and
difficulties on land and sea, he preserves an unshakable
conviction of God's sovereignty, God's providence and God's
love.   But this list also serves to remind us how little of St.
Paul's life we know from the only connected account of it
which we have, the Book of Acts.   Five floggings from the
Jews, two beatings with rods, and three shipwrecks, all of
which happened even before he had visited Jerusalem for
the last time and made his journey to Rome, are known to
us only from this passage.

24. See Deut. 25.1-3; one stripe was omitted in case by a
miscount the Law might be broken.   The Jews were allowed
by the Roman authorities to punish offences against their
Law as long as the punishment did not involve death and
the victim was a Jew.

29. Who is weak
' Who is in danger of sinning, and I am not in sympathy with
him? '

burn not, either (as some commentators say) with indignation, or (as others, taking a much more likely interpretation),

with sympathy and with a desire to help; cf. Rom. 14.13;
I Cor. 8.13.

32. the governor

He was probably an official either supervising the Arab
community in Damascus on behalf of king Aretas, or else
waiting to arrest Paul outside the city. Aretas, a semi-
independent princeling on the edge of the Roman Empire,
was king of Nabataea, and it is unlikely that his territory
included Damascus; he died about 39 A.D.

12.1-10. St. Paul speaks with noticeable restraint and objec-
tivity about his religious experience, here particularly, but
also elsewhere in his letters. For a further treatment of this
subject, see the Note on St. Paul's Conception of the Function of Religious Experience at the end of this Section
(pp. 86-8).

2. man in Christ

Certainly Paul himself; cf. v. 7. Verse 5 is no real contradiction here. If he were to 'glory' about himself, it could
not be about the self who was in Christ.

4. Paradise

The place where the blessed go to dwell with God till the
final Resurrection. It was originally a feature of Iranian
mythology and was pictured as a garden. It is identified or
fused with the garden of Eden in Gen. 2.8ff.; 13.10 and in
Isa. 51.3. In Ezek. 28.13 and 31.8, however, it is thought
of rather as the abode of God (indeed, as the Jews inherited
it, probably the abode of the gods; cf. Isa. 14.13). Our
Lord used the word in the same sense as St. Paul here in
Luke 23.43.[1]

6. St. Paul means that if he were to begin boasting about
his spiritual experiences, his boasts would not be empty ones,
but records of what genuinely happened, perhaps implying
that his opponents' boasts on the same subject were not
genuine.

[1] See Goudge, p. 115.

7. a thorn in the flesh

The word might mean 'stake'. Various guesses as to its meaning have been made, all equally uncertain. In Gal. 4.13-15 Paul recounts how he was afflicted by some physical trouble when he came to the Galatians first, and how they thought nothing of putting him up and would have taken out their own eyes and given them to him had it been possible; it has therefore been conjectured that Paul's eyes were the afflicted part, and that this trouble is what he is alluding to here.

9, 10.

The Interchange of WEAKNESS and STRENGTH is appealed to again (see the Note on this Interchange, pp. 31-3). In Christ, apparent weakness is in fact strength; cf. I Cor. 1.22-31.

9. my grace

Here means 'the *power* imparted by God's gracious act of bringing Paul into Christ', a use of 'grace' not very common in St. Paul's writings, but greatly developed in Christian theology after Paul's day.

that the power of Christ may rest upon me

R.V. Margin, 'cover me'; the Greek, as the R.V. Margin explains, literally means 'tabernacle upon me'. The phrase deliberately recalls the period when the children of Israel in the wilderness brought the Tabernacle with them as the temporary resting-place of God. The Christian Church is now the place where God rests temporarily between the Cross and the End, and the individual Christian is therefore a place where the power of God in Christ may rest (just as the individual Christian is both a stone in the temple of God and himself a temple for the Holy Spirit; Eph. 2.20-22; I Cor. 3.16-17; II Cor. 6.16). St. Paul would have made no distinction between THE POWER OF CHRIST and the Holy Spirit. Cf. John 1.14 ('And the word became flesh and dwelt (literally *tabernacled*) among us, and we beheld his glory '), and I Pet. 4.14 (for the Spirit of glory and the Spirit of God resteth upon you ').

NOTE ON ST. PAUL'S CONCEPTION OF THE FUNCTION OF RELIGIOUS EXPERIENCE

This is one of the very few places where we can be sure that St. Paul is speaking directly of his religious experiences (I Cor. 14.18 is another, and rather startling one). The remarkable feature of it is that though he leaves us in no doubt that he had known profound interior experiences (whether they were technically 'mystical' or not is impossible to determine), and that he was in the habit of receiving direct messages from God in prayer (verse 3; cf. Acts 16.9; 18.9, 10; 27.23, 24), he carefully and deliberately discounts these religious experiences as an argument, and indeed describes such an argument as 'glorying' (II Cor. 12.1). This is in fact characteristic of his normal attitude towards religious experience. Even where in Galatians he describes his own conversion, he refers to it in as objective, almost as impersonal, a way as he can ('But when it pleased God . . . to reveal his Son in me', Gal. 1.15, 16). It is true that he tells us in the same Epistle that he went up to Jerusalem 'by revelation' (2.2), but it is not certain that the revelation was made to him; Acts 11.27-30 would indeed suggest that it was made to Agabus. The evidence therefore of St. Paul's Epistles, taken at least at its face value, points to the conclusion that on the subject of his religious experience St. Paul was remarkably reticent.

The point is worth a special emphasis because it is not one that is usually realized by interpreters of St. Paul's thought. Most expounders of St. Paul assume, consciously or unconsciously, that his beliefs about God's revelation in Christ have been not merely coloured, but almost caused by his religious experience, and some indeed almost suggest that his doctrines were often spun out of his spiritual life, that, for instance, the account of how Christ died for our sins given to us in II Cor. 5 is simply the putting into general and objective terms of the intense spiritual experiences which he enjoyed as he met his Lord in prayer and meditation.

One passage above all in St. Paul's Epistles has appeared to lend support to this conclusion; this is the passage in Galatians which has as its climax the amazing words, ' I am crucified with Christ: nevertheless I live; yet not I, but Christ liveth in me : and the life which I now live in the flesh I live by the faith of the Son of God, who loved me, and gave himself for me ' (Gal. 2.20). Commentator after commentator has in dealing with this passage remarked upon Paul's deep spiritual life and rich mystical experiences; here, they are all quite sure, Paul is reproducing for our inspection the most intimate movements of his soul. So widespread is this conviction, and yet so unsatisfactory, that we must examine the passage more carefully.

In the first place, if this interpretation of the passage were true, Paul would in effect be arguing, ' I have such wonderful religious experiences that I can assure you that Christ is living in me '. This would not only make him unpleasantly resemble a self-righteous boaster (entirely unlike the great Christian men and women of prayer through the ages), but would also directly contradict his refusal in II Cor. 12.1-10 to boast of his religious experience. This is exactly what he would describe as ' foolishness '. But more important than this is the fact that to interpret the statement of Gal. 2.20 as reflecting Paul's interior experiences is to run counter to the context where the verse occurs. The whole point of this passage is that the experience described in Gal. 2.20 must be the experience of *any baptized Christian* (including St. Peter, St. James and even the ' foolish Galatians ' themselves), if the Christian is not in effect to deny his salvation, turn his back on the liberty won for him by Christ, and revert to the Law. To insist upon the observance of the Law as the Galatians have begun to do, as Peter once very unwisely and weakly did, says St. Paul, is to land yourself in the paralysis of Law and sin again. And the proof of this is—not that Paul enjoys the experience of living in Christ, for that is no proof at all—but that *every* Christian has died to the Law when he met Christ in Baptism. Paul's 'I' here is an entirely general 'I', wherein he is taking himself as one example of what happens to everybody, as he similarly instances his own experience in other passages (e.g. Rom. 7; I Cor. 15.29-32).

This is in fact (and here lies the third proof that it is wrong to interpret Gal. 2.20 as primarily a record of Paul's spiritual experience) St. Paul's constant teaching about what happens to baptized Christians. They have been crucified with Christ (Rom. 6.6-9; Col. 3.1-3), and Christ lives in them. The life which they live in the flesh (the part of them which has necessarily to do with creation as yet not wholly redeemed) is still life in Christ, because they live in faith. This is as true of the Corinthians who come drunk to Holy Communion (I Cor. 11.21), and of the women of Philippi who are wrangling with each other (Phil. 4.2, 3), as it is of Paul himself. This is the amazing paradox of Paul's interpretation of Christianity, which is in fact the amazing paradox of the holy God's love for sinful man; and it is not to be explained away in terms of Paul's religious experience.[1]

St. Paul does not of course ignore or belittle religious experience; but he does know the proper place for it to occupy in Christian life and Christian faith. A good example of his handling of this subject is his treatment of 'Speaking with tongues' in I Cor. 14. Christian religious experience is a sign, a consequence and, within clearly understood limits, a guarantee of what has happened to those who have been brought into redeemed relation with God. But one does not found doctrine upon it alone, and one does not allow it to take a prominent place in determining religious thought.

[1] See Rom. 6.1-14; I Cor. 6.12-17 (the Corinthians *are already* ' joined to the Lord ', religious experience or no religious experience); Col. 1.12. 13 ; 2.10-12, 20 ; 3.1-3.

A JUSTIFICATION OF HIS RECENT
ACTIONS AND INTENTIONS
12.11–13.10

12.11. the very chiefest apostles

Not a very good translation, because he probably does
not mean the chief apostles, Peter and James and John,
but his opponents who claim to be their representatives.
R.V. Margin's rendering, 'those pre-eminent apostles',
or the Revised Standard Version, 'these superlative
apostles', importing a note of sarcasm into the phrase, is
better.

12. the signs of an apostle

Obviously set the apostle apart as one quite different from
others and not, at least in this respect, capable of handing
on his peculiar endowments (see the Note on Apostleship,
pp. 57-62). But see Gal. 6.17 for different signs of an
apostle.

14. The first time Paul came to the Corinthians was presumably when he came to evangelize them; the second time
when he paid them a short and hurried, and most unsatisfactory visit, just before this letter was written (see 2.1). In
13.1 he refers to these two visits again. It is probably because he so emphatically declared his intention of visiting
Corinth again soon in this letter that in his next letter (preserved in II Cor. 1.1–9.15) he takes so much trouble to
justify his later decision not to pay this early visit (cf.
1.15-18; 2.1-13 and see the Introduction, pp. 10-14, and the
note on 1.15, p. 33).

15. It is better to end this verse with a question (as do R.V.,
Revised Standard Version and Moffatt), and translate:
'If I have loved you more abundantly, am I to be less
loved?'

16. He states the next objection to his conduct which he is going to meet.

18. I desired Titus

Should be: 'I urged Titus to go', as translated by the Revised Standard Version. We do not of course know who the BROTHER was. There is some difficulty in envisaging when exactly this visit of Titus can have taken place. It can hardly have been the visit mentioned in 2.13; 7.6, 13, because we have assumed that this was the visit on which Titus carried the 'Severe Letter' and at which the Corinthians' change of heart took place and therefore after the writing of this passage. It is even less likely to have been the visit mentioned in 8.6, 17, 18, 22, because this is apparently yet to take place when that part of II Corinthians was written (later than this passage) and was for the purpose of extracting money for the Collection. It is very likely to have been the visit mentioned in 8.6, earlier than either of the other two, at which Titus initiated the Collection; this would fit in with the defensive tone which Paul adopts in referring to him and with the mention of making A GAIN in v. 17 (see the Introduction, p. 22).

19. It is not certain that this sentence should in fact be a question. It could run: 'you have all the time been thinking that we are excusing ourselves.'

20. swellings

'Conceit' is better.

21. my God will humble me

Either because Paul will have to speak sternly to the Corinthians, and this will humiliate him; or else (more likely) because to discover such odious sins among those whom he has spiritually begotten (see v. 14, and cf. Gal. 4.19; I Cor. 4.14, 15) is naturally humiliating. It is noteworthy that the sort of sins that St. Paul lists here are those peculiarly to which people who prided themselves on their spiritual achievement and knowledge and wisdom might give way. It is obvious from I Corinthians that the Corinthians did imagine themselves to possess such special gifts (I Cor. 1.19–2.5; 3.18-19; 4.10; 8.1-3; 12.1-31; 13.2; 14.1, 37-40).

13.3-4. The final reference to the Interchange of weakness and strength in the apostle of Jesus Christ. The same theme has been touched on in I Cor. 1.22–2.5; 4.10-13. And there, as here, Paul finally refuses to make claims or substantiate his authority by relying on positive advantages possessed by him, a dominating personality, or extraordinary spiritual experiences, or the capacity to work wonders; he falls back for his authority simply on the fact that the weakness of Christ his Master is reproduced in him. It is another way of saying 'From henceforth let no man trouble me; for I bear in my body the marks of the Lord Jesus' (Gal. 6.17). The strength of the Lord Jesus Christ, from whom his opponents too were always demanding a sign (Matt. 12.38ff.; 16.1ff.; Mark 8.11ff.; Luke 11.29ff.), lay wholly in his weakness, that is, in the complete pouring out of himself in obedience to the will of God (see Phil. 2.5-11).

5-7. The words PROVE YOUR OWN SELVES, REPROBATES and APPROVED all come from the same root in Greek and they point to a fundamental conviction of St. Paul, that men and women who are 'in Christ' have God's approval (which is another way of putting the more technical phrase, 'are justified in God's sight'). But at the same time, as long as they are in this mortal body they are also 'on approval' before God. No man can be quite certain that God's *final* approval will be given to him (see I Cor. 3.10-15; II Cor. 5.10; Rom. 14.10); Paul even in one passage says that he cannot be sure that he will gain this final approval himself (I Cor. 9.27). In the particular passage concerned here Paul implies a contrast between the approval of God and the

approval of men. St. Paul may be REPROBATE to the Corinthians (the Revised Standard Version takes this very
technical sounding phrase as equivalent to 'having failed to
pass the test '); he may have failed to pass the Corinthians'
test. But he knows that he is APPROVED by God in his
dealings with the Christians of Corinth, and he is more
anxious as to whether they are properly concerned about
their state of 'approval', about the possibility of their
not having passed God's test (see v. 7). St. Paul is
even willing to appear to them not to have passed
the test, if he can only rouse them to consider their own
condition.

But Christians, according to St. Paul, are subject to a
double 'approval'; not only is God 'proving' them, but they
can and should 'prove' what is the will of God. They can
do this because they live in the New Creation, because they
possess the Spirit and live in faith (I Cor. 2.6-16; Rom. 12.2;
Phil. 1.10). They can also 'prove' themselves, for the same
reasons, as St. Paul urges them to do here (cf. I Cor. 11.28;
Gal. 6.4). 'For as touching brotherly love ye need not that
I write unto you: for ye yourselves are taught of God to
love one another', he says to the Christians of Thessalonica
(I Thess. 4.9). Christians have been given by God a spiritual
insight whereby they can know God's will for themselves
and in some measure determine their own spiritual condition as those who are not Christians cannot. They
can, in G. K. Chesterton's words, 'walk with clearer
eyes and ears this path that wandereth'; they can 'see
undrugged', in spite of the many opiates provided by
modern society.

Two more points must be made about this important
passage. First of all REPROBATE does not necessarily mean
destined from eternity to hell ', as it came to mean in certain
much later developments of Christian theology. In Paul's
letters it means no more than 'having failed to qualify for
inclusion in God's redeeming plan '. This state is the
opposite of being IN THE FAITH (v. 5), which does not mean

'having accepted the doctrines of orthodox Christianity', but living in the new atmosphere or universe which inclusion in Christ's Body brings with it.

Secondly, this passage presents us with the question, How can the Corinthians know that they are APPROVED or IN THE FAITH? Can they do it by appealing to their religious experience? There is no satisfactory support for this view in St. Paul's letters. What Paul means when he urges the Corinthians to PROVE themselves is that he wants them to ask themselves whether their behaviour has been entirely consistent with their redeemed status. Christian behaviour is the test of whether Christians are APPROVED or not. A good example of this occurs in II Cor. 2.9 where Paul implies that the test of being 'approved' for the Corinthians is whether they are obedient to him; perhaps he had his warning about God's 'approval', given in II Cor. 12.5-7, in mind when he wrote II Cor. 2.9. An example of a situation where a Christian would have to be regarded as REPROBATE is found in I Cor. 6, where it is likely that Paul hopes that the offender will finally return into the faith again (for similar appeals to his hearers to examine themselves see Rom. 6.11-13; I Cor. 5.8-11; 11.27-32; Col. 3.1-8). A Christian's conduct, then, is a very good ready reckoner for determining his relationship to Christ, and a much better one than his religious experience.

But note that we must say, 'a *Christian's* conduct'. Neither this passage nor any other passage in St. Paul's letters gives the slightest justification for imagining that what matters is how good you are, not how religious you are (the illusion, roughly speaking, of the average Englishman). St. Paul in fact says precisely the opposite; he says that all the noble and decent conduct of all the good men in the world does not justify even one of them in the eyes of God. Unless you have died with Christ, unless you have been united with him in baptism and live in him by faith, unless you have been brought into this saving relationship with God, no goodness will save you. Your *goodness* will not indeed save you when you are in this relationship, but once you have been given it in baptism and accepted it in faith your conduct is a good rule of thumb for judging how far the relationship is being maintained on your side. Our behaviour, in short, is the test of our nearness to God, but not the cause of it.

10. In this last sentence of the ' Severe Letter ' as we know it, St. Paul reverts to the phrase which he used earlier in the letter (10.8). The Lord has given him authority and he will not hesitate to use it constructively. It is a salutary and appropriate note upon which to end a study of II Corinthians, not only because the Epistle is very largely concerned with the subject of authority, but because authority in the Church is a matter upon which a great deal of muddled thinking is current to-day. We live in an age which is almost hypnotically dominated by a reverence for democracy. We assume almost unconsciously that the only way for any institution to be governed is by a majority of votes. All social and political activities are conditioned by the recognition that each individual possesses a number of fundamental rights which must on no account be violated. Democracy shouts at us from advertisements, regulates us in our ration-books, preaches at us over the radio. It has even invaded the Church in the form of Assemblies, Conferences and Convocations, no doubt very much to the Church's benefit. It is therefore very difficult for us to recognize that in the New Testament conception of the place of authority in the Church there is not the faintest resemblance to any modern democratic theory whatever. This is not really surprising, because the Christian Church grew up in a civilization which had comparatively recently witnessed the pathetic failure of the Greek city states and was itself only slowly recovering from the effects of the terrifying failure of the democracy of the Roman Republic. So emphatic had been the failure of both that no state in Europe was to experiment in democracy until well over a thousand years after St. Paul's day.

In the New Testament there is only one source of authority in the Church—the Lord Jesus Christ. He confers this authority upon his apostles who, vested with this authority, have an entire right to the obedience of their converts. The authority of the apostle of Jesus Christ is not exclusive; other people bear their measure of authority for their various functions, prophets, teachers, healers, administrators, interpreters of ecstatic utterance (I Cor. 12.28-30; Eph. 4.11, 12). And the Holy Spirit is not bound to Holy Orders; he can raise up people like Cornelius (Acts 10), and Agabus (Acts 11.27-28; 21.10-11) independently of them. But the chief authority in the Church lies with the apostle of Jesus Christ, authority to evangelize, to direct and be overseer of the newly-formed Christian communities, authority to initiate action and make policy, authority also to admit to the fellowship of the Church and to cast out from it. Such a situation is dimly visible in the Book of Acts and meets us clearly and unmistakably in the First and Second Epistles to the Corinthians. There is no hint anywhere that the collective will of the majority of individual Christians in the whole Church or in any local church bears of itself any authority. Authority in the Church is exercised by Jesus Christ, expressing himself through various agents for various purposes, but chiefly through his apostles. The authority of the apostolic ministry must by its very nature be capable of being handed on, or it is hard to see how the historical existence of the Church could continue.

How that handing on is contrived, and who are the people who bear the authority of the apostolic ministry to-day, are questions upon which it is beyond the scope of this work to enter. It is enough to indicate that to refuse to take this apostolic ministry seriously as part of the Christian gospel, as an essential ingredient of the Christian Church, is to run counter to the convictions of the New Testament. And to envisage this ministry as in some way appertaining to the rights and privileges of every baptized Christian, or to regard the apostle of Jesus Christ as merely a chosen representative of the Christian community, local or universal, is equally unscriptural. The apostolic minister, to-day as in St. Paul's day, is in his apostolic functions not merely an ecclesiastical M.P. He is an agent of the Lord Jesus Christ, from whom alone he derives his authority to govern and tend the flock of his Lord, *to build up and not to pull down.*